THE DECK OF LIFE

THE DECK OF LIFE
PLAYING THE CARDS YOU'RE DEALT

RICHARD J. FERRARA SR., MD

iUniverse, Inc.
New York   Bloomington

THE DECK OF LIFE
PLAYING THE CARDS YOU'RE DEALT

iUniverse books may be ordered through booksellers or by contacting:

iUniverse
1663 Liberty Drive
Bloomington, IN 47403
www.iuniverse.com
1-800-Authors (1-800-288-4677)

Because of the dynamic nature of the Internet, any Web addresses or links contained in this book may have changed since publication and may no longer be valid. The views expressed in this work are solely those of the author and do not necessarily reflect the views of the publisher, and the publisher hereby disclaims any responsibility for them.

ISBN: 978-0-595-48061-6 (sc)
ISBN: 978-0-595-61143-0 (dj)
ISBN: 978-0-595-60158-5 (ebk)

Printed in the United States of America

iUniverse rev. date: 11/23/2009

Acknowledgments

Many physicians that I have befriended in the past impacted my spiritual and scientific beliefs. One of the first and most important was Dr. Paul Tournier, author, physician, and founder of the Society for the Whole Person in Europe. Others who played an important role were Dr. Patrick Vilani, Dr. Walter Levick, Dr. Maxwell Gardener, and Dr. Lee Carrick, all of whom were prominent physicians in Grosse Pointe, Michigan.

This book is a creation that evolved over many years of my life. Early in my medical education, a sense of spirituality, along with a scientific awareness, kindled a curiosity to search for meanings and truths in life. My natural calling toward a love of people and nature led me to my chosen field of dermatology following my studies in internal medicine. All of my experiences, both pleasant and painful, seemed to reveal a meaning and purpose. This sparked a desire to share these experiences with others. Early in my medical career, I began to delve into literature involving the whole person—body, mind, and spirit. The study of dermatology seemed to lend itself to my pursuit of understanding the whole person. My observations reflected genetic predispositions in virtually all known human conditions and ailments, whether their origin be physical, mental, or spiritual. These interests led me to seek knowledge of medical history, ancient and modern philosophy, religion, and spiritual forces. A host of other people began to appear in my life whose influence formulated who I am today.

A patient and evangelist, Rev. Achilles Myers, introduced Dr. Paul Tournier to me through his books. Dr. Tournier and I subsequently became friends. Father Joseph Dustin was a dear friend, spiritualist, and outstanding banjoist who had a profound effect on the development of my spiritual and musical life. Judith Persing was important among countless others who encouraged me and acted as teachers. I truly offer my humble gratitude for their lessons. My secretary and confidant, Mary Daniels, did a superb job in deciphering my handwritten text, correcting my grammatical errors, and simplifying my writing for the reader's ease. My spiritual friend Earlene McMillen of Grosse Pointe, Michigan, helped me organize this book and edited the first draft.

My heartfelt gratitude goes out to my daughter Virginia Ferrara Twaits for her artistic contributions, and to my daughter Linda Lantz for her computer assistance. I give thanks for my grandsons, Richard and Christopher Tarjeft, for their painstaking graphic illustrations and computer assistance. Lastly, I would like to thank my dear wife, Joan Ferrara, for her patience, goodness, support, and assistance in the completion of this book.

Contents

PART TWO

DISEASE PREDISPOSITIONS OF THE FOUR TEMPERAMENTS

PART THREE

PRACTICAL APPLICATIONS OF THE TEMPERAMENT THEORY

PART FOUR

DISCOVER AND BALANCE YOUR TEMPERAMENT

PART FIVE

BIRTH OF A NEW ERA

CHARTS AND DIAGRAMS

Introduction

The Resurgence of the Hippocrates Temperament Theory

During my early years of medical practice as a dermatologist, a patient who was an evangelistic minister gave me a book titled *A Whole Person in a Broken World*. This book was written by Dr. Paul Tournier, a French-Swiss physician, philosopher, historian, theologian, and founder of the Society for Medicine of the Whole Person in Europe. I seriously studied this book and was intrigued with Dr. Tournier's wisdom. I subsequently made a special trip to Geneva, Switzerland, in 1967 to meet Dr. Tournier personally, and he ignited my interest in writing this book.

After graduating from Northwestern Medical School, and having acquired several postgraduate degrees in medicine and board certification in dermatology, I felt well prepared to pursue my chosen field of dermatology. Until I read Dr. Tournier's book, I was not aware that Western medicine had been based on Hippocrates' temperament theory for more than two thousand years. This theory subscribes to four temperaments and their humors (relating to body fluids and functions). It encompasses Hippocrates' philosophy of character and health and describes the integral nature of body, mind, and spirit. Unfortunately, this knowledge of the temperament theory has been essentially ignored in modern medical education for the last one hundred years.

Around the beginning of the twentieth century, the research and theories of Sigmund Freud started a new concept in the study of personality and personality disorders. He and his advocates persisted in implementing a deterministic point of view stating that man is a victim of his environment and that man's environment determines his behavior. This behavior concept weakened and almost discredited the theory of the four temperaments, as it claimed to speak in the name of science. Only a few firm believers of the temperament theory openly questioned the validity of the Freudian theory.

Over the last several decades, there has been a significant reawakening of interest in ancient wisdom. Many people are realizing that, in spite of technological advances, our problems have not lessened, stresses seem to have increased, and there is a prevalent feeling of personal and mass despair. People are beginning to contemplate that perhaps nutrition and spiritual and undiscovered forces play an integral part in the life of the whole person. Today's generation is more concerned about the meaning of things like physiological mechanisms, not just their scientific classifications and explanations. Many are rejecting medical manipulations of bodily functions by drugs, surgery, chemotherapy, and radiation as the only method of treatment of disease, and are embracing alternative methods of treatment, especially involving nutrition and spiritual influences, both modern and ancient. This interest has given rise to a new medical field called *integrative medicine,* which acknowledges all the alternative methods of healing for the maintenance and wellness of the whole person—body, mind, and spirit.

Constitutional Medicine

The resurrection of this fascinating subject and its relationship to the temperament theory led me to investigate, and eventually conclude, after many years in medical practice, that the art of observation combined with knowledge of the four temperaments reveals a definite association between body build, personality, and the predisposition to certain diseases. This is known as *constitutional medicine,* which is defined as the art of clinical observation that acknowledges this association in the diagnosis of disease. Astute clinicians have recognized and utilized this association since antiquity. Unfortunately, rapid medical advances and the introduction of technology in the diagnosis of disease have led to a marked decline in interest in constitutional medicine today.

Although my observations of hundreds of patients are considered anecdotal, they do not conflict with any modern scientific studies. In fact, much of contemporary science affirms the reality of the theory of the four temperaments, which when in balance create health, peace, and harmony, and when out of balance create illness, pain, and disharmony.

Around the same time that I was exploring Dr. Tournier's work, I read two significant books by W. H. Sheldon, PhD, MD, related to body build, temperament, and disease predisposition. In *The Varieties of Human Physique* and *The Varieties of Temperament,* Dr. Sheldon attempted to scientifically authenticate the validity of this relationship with exhaustive studies of more than four thousand college-age students. (A more detailed presentation of his work is included in chapter V.) I also read *Physique and Character* by Dr. Ernst Kretschmer, whose book describes his study of several hundred inmates of mental institutions in Germany to determine the relationship between measurements of human physiques and mental and physical illness. These distinguished authors reinforced my resolve to observe and record studies that I felt would support my conviction about the relationship between temperament, physique, personality, and predisposition to illness.

Methodology of Study

In my early studies, I confined my attention to the study of the relationship between temperament and skin disease. Having been trained in both dermatology and internal medicine, my interest soon expanded to include internal diseases and disorders as well.

My method of study consisted of an initial clinical diagnosis of the temperament blend in the individual patient. Based on my clinical observations and my knowledge of the four temperaments, I devised a formula to indicate the order sequence of their temperament blend from the strongest to the weakest. The choleric, sanguine, melancholic, and phlegmatic temperaments were represented by C, S, M, and P, respectively. The first letter in my formula represented the most dominant temperament, and the last letter represented that least observed in the patient. Later, I will discuss in detail the psychological, physiological, and physical characteristics of each temperament. For now, a brief description associated with the representative first letter is presented to facilitate learning. These descriptions are the essential features of each temperament as originally described by Hippocrates.

The choleric temperament (C)

- Predominance of the bones, musculature, and extremities.
- Athletic build.
- Characterized by aggressiveness and physical hyperactivity.
- Associated with the element fire and the body humor yellow bile.

The sanguine temperament (S)

- Predominance of the upper trunk and respiratory and circulatory systems.
- Characterized by likeable, extroversive personality and inflated optimism.
- Associated with the element air and the body humor blood.

The melancholic temperament (M)

- Predominance of the lower trunk, abdomen, and digestive system.
- Characterized by creativeness and emotional sensitivity.
- Associated with the element earth and the body humor black bile.

The phlegmatic temperament (P)

- Predominance of the nervous system and a general diminished development of all parts of the body.
- Characterized by appearing passive, easygoing, and well-balanced.
- Associated with the element water and the body humor lymph.

Although we are all a blend of the four temperaments, for all practical purposes, only two (dominant and secondary subdominant temperaments) are clinically discernable in each person.

After evaluating the person clinically and ascertaining the individual's formula, I asked the patient to complete a personality test to determine the sequence of their temperaments. The psychological test was devised by Florence Littauer in her book *Personality Plus,* and is reprinted in chapter III. I was surprised to achieve approximately 80 percent accuracy when comparing my initial clinical observation formula with the results of the psychological tests. With this information and a physical examination of each patient, I concluded that there is a strong tendency toward specific diseases in each of the four temperaments.

Again, the methodology used in this study was primarily anecdotal and certainly does not meet the strict criteria of scientific methodology. No human system is perfect, even when studied using the widely accepted scientific method. However, comprehending and acknowledging the values of the temperament theory will help people understand themselves and others. Strengths can be maximized and promoted, and weaknesses can be strengthened, to make life more healthy, more pleasant, and less stressful.

Nurture versus Nature

After forty years of clinical practice and observation, much of the medical community has come to realize that even though the genetic code determines features relating to body build, temperament, and disease predisposition, people also have an inherent ability to alter these features by their belief system. In other words, the genetic code or DNA is essentially a blueprint of a person, but does not in itself direct behavior. Personal characteristics, behavior, and reactions to life's situations are governed by what beliefs are stored in the subconscious mind. Literature on positive thinking has added meaning and validity to the universal law of attraction that affirms, "You receive what you believe."

Dr. Bruce Lipton, a cellular biologist, has made breakthrough discoveries in this area. In his recent book *The Biology of Belief,* he clearly demonstrates the association between mind and matter. He reveals how the influence of thought perception and subconscious awareness can alter one's body-healing potential, and he uncovers the connection between biology, psychology, and spirituality. Dr. Lipton confirms that we are not victims of our genes, but instead have an unlimited capacity to live a life of peace, happiness, health, and love. He presents solid evidence that our beliefs create every aspect of our personal reality and dispels the myth of genetic determinism. His contribution on the belief system will be discussed in more detail in chapter XI.

Purpose of This Book

This book was inspired by reviewing past and present pertinent literature on the temperaments along with my own personal documentations and clinical observations of hundreds of patients in my medical practice. It was inspired by my meeting with Dr. Tournier, who motivated my interest in the temperament theory, and by my own increased sensitivity to signs and symptoms of disease in my patients.

Initially, my interest was to investigate the impact of emotional and spiritual conflicts on skin diseases. Dr. Tournier approved of my project and suggested a theme, "When the spirit is disturbed, the skin cries." Because of my interest and training in both internal medicine and dermatology, I chose to investigate the whole person from this standpoint.

I became increasingly aware of the influence of genetics, mental attitude, and spiritual factors on the development of disease and concluded that, in general, three observations hold true: (1) those patients who are alike physically tend to act alike; (2) a definite type of body build seems to be associated with a certain type of personality; and (3) there appears to be a definite relationship between body build, personality, and disease predisposition. Observation revealed that certain patterns of disease appeared to be associated with each dominant temperament. This awareness directed me to be more specific in counseling my patients and led me to the desire to share this information.

Dr. Tournier once related to me the true role of the physician: the physician occasionally cures, and he frequently relieves pain and suffering, but he *always* listens, consoles, and correctly advises on the prevention of disease.

In summary, this book presents information on the history of the temperament theory beginning with Hippocrates and includes prevalent research on the subject. It offers a personality profile test to aid the reader in determining his or her own personal temperament. Suggestions on strengthening weaknesses and using one's strengths to change undesirable behavior are offered. The disease predispositions within each temperament are discussed, along with how this knowledge can help the reader improve his or her own health. Every person can modify his or her temperament through knowledge, self-discovery, and the promotion of spiritual values.

The title of this book, *The Deck of Life*, was selected mainly because of the analogy to a deck of cards, which reflects the meaning and nature of the book. In the card game of bridge, as in life, we are dealt a hand that we must understand and manage to achieve the best possible outcome. In the bridge game, a thirteen-card hand is dealt to each of four players, usually consisting of a mixture of the four suits. The occurrence of a hand consisting of just one suit is extremely rare, and one with just two suits or three suits is infrequent. The four suits are like the four temperaments and vary in strength from the strongest to the weakest in the following order: spades (♠) represents the choleric (strongest), hearts (♥) represents sanguine, diamonds (♦) represents melancholic, and clubs (♣) represents phlegmatic (weakest). The first two are considered aggressive temperaments, and the last two are considered passive temperaments. The number and strength of each suit are evaluated to determine how best to bid and manage the hand dealt to you in the card game and in life. The hand dealt in cards occurs as a random chance, whereas the hand dealt in life is predetermined by a specific inherited genetic code (DNA) that has an ancestral influence. The chance of an exact replication of the hand dealt is infinitesimal in cards, and even more so in nature.

Successful management of the hand dealt in bridge and in life depends on knowledge, experience, intentional thought, and belief to secure a balance with the fullest potential. Without balance, failure, disease, stress, suffering, and unfulfilled potential most likely will ensue. This book deals with the proper recognition and knowledge of your inherited nature (predominant temperament) and how to achieve balance in life by promoting your strengths and correcting your weaknesses in body, mind, and spirit. This holistic approach can lead to a healthy, happier life with longevity and fulfillment of one's potential.

PART ONE

THE HIPPOCRATES FOUR TEMPERAMENTS AND BLENDS

Chapter I

The Four Temperaments (Personality Types)

Introduction to the Four Temperaments

The study and applications of the four temperaments and their associations is not currently supported with exact scientific data. Nevertheless, the practical application of this knowledge is an art based on astute clinical observations that encompass all the human faculties of the senses and intuition.

Anyone interested in learning to be perceptive in observing humans could use this knowledge to understand themselves and others, thus improving relationships. This would be especially valuable to such professionals as priests, ministers, psychologists, social workers, teachers, and artists. Knowledge of individual temperaments and this method of introspection can assist you in improving your self-image, and will aid in all aspects of life including romance, marriage, raising children, choosing a career, employing and working with others, selecting hobbies, and choosing a proper diet. In general, it provides a whole new meaning to life for a healthier body, mind, and spirit.

This chapter will be devoted to describing in depth the four temperaments as initially discerned by Hippocrates. As stated earlier, he divided people into four basic types: choleric, sanguine, melancholic, and phlegmatic. Each temperament type has naturally inherent strong and weak tendencies. Because all individuals are genetically made up of a mixture of the four basic types, the resultant temperament will be primarily determined by the most dominant inherited traits.

This system of utilizing knowledge of the four temperaments is not exact because the inherent features in human nature vary in degrees so that no one individual is an exact replica of another. For all practical purposes, however, an astute observer can determine the dominant and subdominant temperament and then confirm this relative diagnosis with psychological testing. This knowledge enables an interested person to diagnose his or her own temperament type, and thus be aware of inherited strengths and weaknesses. One will then be better equipped to take advantage of the natural strengths and learn to correct the natural weaknesses to keep from thwarting one's innate potential and creativity in life. We must recognize that no one is perfectly balanced; each strength is most likely counterbalanced with an equally potent weakness. When reading over the descriptions of the four temperaments, it is easy to identify with one of them. It is natural to gloat over the strengths, but then find the weaknesses distasteful and unacceptable. This may even cause one to reject any further study. It is important that we face reality and unmask and correct our weaknesses. This will help us better understand ourselves and others and enjoy a more fruitful life.

As mentioned earlier, Hippocrates associated each of the four temperaments with one of the four specific universal elements (fire, air, earth, and water) and with one of the seasons (spring, summer, fall, and winter). He also associated the four temperaments with functions of specific body fluids that he called humors: yellow bile, blood, black bile, and lymph. These associations are demonstrated in Chart 1 with the commonly used substitute descriptive terms that have evolved over the centuries.

Chart 1
Descriptive Terms Related to the Elements and Humors

Choleric (Summer)	Sanguine (Spring)	Melancholic (Autumn)	Phlegmatic (Winter)
Element—Fire	**Element**—Air	**Element**—Earth	**Element**—Water
Descriptive Terms Fireball Hell-bent Hot-headed Speed demon	**Descriptive Terms** High flyer Optimist Full of air	**Descriptive Terms** Nature lover Meditator Pessimist Environmentalist	**Descriptive Terms** Easygoing Even-tempered Nice guy Peacemaker
Humor—Yellow Bile (gallbladder fluid)	**Humor**—Blood	**Humor**—Black Bile (lower bowel fluid)	**Humor**—Lymph
Descriptive Terms Gutsy A lot of gall Intestinal fortitude Aggressive	**Descriptive Terms** Big-hearted Lover Warm teddy bear Red hot mama Giver (like Santa)	**Descriptive Terms** Loner Downer Recluse Daydreamer Oddball Weird Nerd	**Descriptive Terms** Content Procrastinator Hypochondriac Funny guy Couch potato

Each temperament appears to have preferences in the type of music, songs, and instruments that they enjoy. Chart 2 illustrates these preferences.

Chart 2
Preferred Music and Instruments among the Temperaments

	Choleric	Sanguine	Melancholic	Phlegmatic
Preferred Music	Marching Patriotic College fight songs Hard rock	Happy Upbeat Cheerful Love songs	Classical Meditative Reflective Blues	Slow Lazy Dreamy River, water songs
Examples	Air Corps Song "Stars and Stripes" "Born to Be Wild" "Battle Hymn of the Republic"	"Hello, Dolly" "You Are My Sunshine" "When You're Smiling" "People Who Need People"	"Phantom of the Opera" "Melancholy Baby" "Good-bye Sunshine" "Yesterday"	"Lonely" "Lonesome Me" "Let It Be" "Me and My Shadow" "All by Myself"
Preferred Instruments	Steel guitar Drums Trumpet Any percussion	Piano (jazz) Banjo Tuba Xylophone Accordion	Piano (classical) Violin Flute Classical Strings Cello Harp	Clarinet Saxophone Acoustical guitar Ukulele Harmonica

Each temperament has the tendency to own certain types of pets, especially dogs that are similar to their own nature. The choleric may prefer outdoor, running, hyperactive dogs like the German shepherd, the border collie, or any hunting dog. The sanguine may prefer loveable and lap type dogs. The melancholic may prefer passive dogs of beauty and grace like the golden retriever or Labrador. The phlegmatic would be attracted to the quiet, obedient, and more passive dog.

1. The Choleric Temperament

Strengths

The basic strengths of the choleric temperament are characterized by being strong-willed, self-disciplined, practical, and a natural leader with self-confidence and optimism. Another outstanding trait of the choleric is a powerful self-determination when taking on a project. The choleric is confident, frequently arrogant, decisive, and tends to be aggressive in actions. They are often flamboyant, with a preference for red colors. Their projects are generally well planned with a practical or useful purpose.

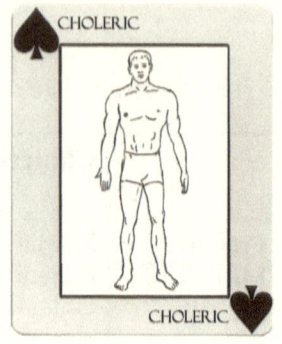

Cholerics are usually tenacious and persistent in one direction and most often accomplish their goals successfully. In all aspects of life they are practical and appear to be happiest when engaged in a useful project. They excel in leadership and organizational abilities, although they dislike and delegate the detail work. The choleric is superior in evaluating problems and advising practical solutions in management. Most often these decisions are spontaneously made and appear to be more intuitive than the product analytical reasoning. Their strong leadership abilities make cholerics especially qualified in business, politics, the military, the judicial system, the police force, sports, and in any position requiring quick, competitive, bold, or fearless action.

Cholerics are naturally self-confident, ambitious, and optimistic in all adventures they may undertake. They are usually endowed with a keen intelligence although rarely brilliant. Their pioneer spirit and adventuresome and masculine nature created the image of the western man who fought the Indians and settled the western wilderness of early America.

Weaknesses

Weaknesses of the choleric temperament are mainly related to the hard, stern, angry, impetuous, decisive, and self-sufficient traits. They have good reasoning ability, but tend to be deficient in imagination, creative ideas, and emotions. Choleric men rarely cry after adolescence, and anyone with an effeminate, sentimental, or crying disposition is usually repugnant to them. Choleric women only cry when facing desperate circumstances or from self-pity. They can be hard, heartless, even cruel and abusive in the treatment of others. They find it difficult to apologize or show approval to one they have offended. Instead, they may even repeat their offense with a sarcastic tongue.

These characteristics can produce anguish and poor self-image in the spouse of a choleric person.

Cholerics are inclined to be hot-tempered and can become furious in an instant. After exploding in anger, they often continue to carry a grudge and can even be revengeful. Their disposition may reveal anger, pride, stubbornness, and a highly opinionated nature. This could cause much discomfort and distress in those that work or live with them. They often feel unloved without realizing that they must give love to receive love. Their tendency to be cruel is manifested in their subconscious desire to dominate others and render them subservient. A strong ego, self-will, and haughty persistence may lead them to practice hypocrisy, deception, and even outright dishonesty rather than concede to weakness or defeat.

Habits and Social Traits of the Choleric

The choleric nature is to save time and accomplish as much as possible in a given period. This is clearly evident in most habits and social traits. The choleric usually arrives early and is never late. They often lead the discussion and get to the issue quickly, primarily with underlying self-interest.

They seldom change their diet, mostly preferring soups, meat, and potatoes. In their eating habits, they tend to take large chunks of food, eat quickly, and talk while chewing. They are usually the first to finish a meal.

Cholerics tend to be daring drivers, risk takers, and speed demons. They constantly dart in and out of traffic. By driving aggressively, they feel they are saving time. They are not casual shoppers and prefer to go quickly to a specific store to purchase something they need. When they must shop, they usually overbuy.

The majority of cholerics excel in academics. They often prefer social subjects, such as history, geography, literature, and psychology. Many are speed readers and have inquisitive minds. They generally skim over things quickly and may not be good spellers. They like graphic illustrations and visual aids showing the relationships between things, and they prefer to stay on one topic without deviation. Cholerics do not take the time to write legibly, resulting in poor handwriting.

Cholerics are extroverts to the extent of speaking freely and deliberately. They are generally very proficient in debates and arguments. They have a great need to be right in their assertions, which can lead to a false sense of righteousness and pride.

They are timely and orderly in paying bills, but they dislike balancing their own checkbook, so they will readily accept bank statements.

In raising children, choleric parents usually exercise strong authority and run their household with firm discipline. Their children are raised by strict rules and regulations. They tend to overreact in correcting their children and may spank too often and too hard. Their tone of voice is loud, and they give direct orders in a stern manner. Cholerics make good strong parents, but they are difficult to please and they rarely offer approval, which can make their children feel inferior and rejected.

2. The Sanguine Temperament

Strengths

The strong points of the sanguine are character-ized by the following features: love and joy in all aspects of life; a cheery, friendly, uplifting opti-mism that is contagious to others; and a giving, compassionate nature of goodness in communi-cating with others.

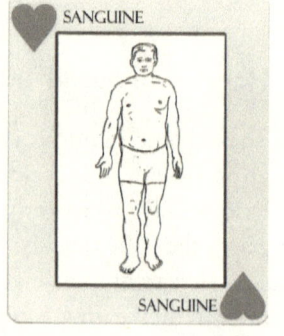

The love of life is evident in the sanguine's childlike curiosity about things. They often rise early in the morning in a cheerful mood, singing and whistling. Sanguines usually maintain a happy disposition and are seldom bored. Discouraging events or solemn news are quickly forgotten as they turn to some fascinating or enlightening thought. They portray optimism for the future but live in the present. They do not readily plan ahead and are easily distracted and inspired by new projects and friends. Their cheerful, friendly nature is displayed in handshaking, touching, and their genuine love for people.

Sanguines liven up a party, taking care to include people who appear to not be enjoying themselves. Their love and concern for people and their charismatic manner are almost always returned. They are responsive to the needs of others and share in their emotional experiences, both good and bad, with compassion. Other temperaments often misinterpret or doubt the sincerity of the sanguine. Because they often unintentionally live in the present and not the past, no one can love you more and forget you faster than the sanguine temperament.

Because sanguines are such people persons, they function well in public relations, as personal receptionists, and in sales.

Weaknesses

The basic weaknesses of the sanguine include restlessness, having a weak will, being egotistical, and revealing emotional instability. Their restlessness is evident in their endless activities, which are often impractical and disorganized. Their emotional nature leads them to become instantly excited, which can cause them to run haphazardly in the wrong direction. Their restlessness also leads to difficulty in concentration, which may prevent them from excelling in scholastics or in their careers.

Because of their exuberant personality, sanguines are often voted "most likely to succeed," and yet they often fail. Their pursuits often change direction, and, therefore, they tend not to measure up to their potential. More often than not, their greatest problems are being weak-willed and undisciplined, both of which are hidden by their dynamic personality. They have a great need to be loved and accepted and will frequently compromise themselves to that end. Exaggerating, denying, or stretching the truth is common behavior.

Sanguines are notorious for initiating projects and never finishing them. If they are approached for any service, they instantly respond favorably without considering the time, abilities, and other responsibilities the task may entail. They love to please others and do not know their own limitations. It is difficult for them to do the necessary preparatory work on any project without the stimulus of a group. They may easily forget their resolutions, appointments, or obligations unintentionally, and have a tendency to be undependable when it comes to time schedules or deadlines. For these reasons, sanguines often fail to meet their commitments.

The loveable, loving sanguines are prone to problems of lust since they are such touchy-feely people. They are often faced with sexual temptation and may find it difficult to resist.

Egotism often appears early in life, which makes a sanguine seem more mature for his or her age. They may act obnoxious by interrupting and dominating conversations. As they become older, talking about self and their own interests dominates conversations with others.

Emotional instability is evident in the sanguine by how easily they cry from an emotional situation, discouragement, or feeling sorry for themselves. Their warm nature can produce spontaneous anger and verbal lashings quickly. They explode and then forget about it quickly, not realizing that others don't. They never seem to worry about their outbursts but readily apologize for them, often repeating them over and over.

Habits and Social Traits of the Sanguine

The sanguine is often late for appointments and readily makes rational excuses for their tardiness. Before addressing the primary purpose of the appointment they will frequently talk profusely on unrelated subjects, such as weather, friends, or events.

Sanguines tend to eat greedily and indulge in most available foods, which is probably why they are prone to obesity. In a restaurant, they frequently talk and ignore the menu until after the waiter arrives for the order. Their preferred menu usually includes breads, fats, creamy foods, and shellfish. They favor beer or wine over hard liquor.

The sanguine is an erratic driver, sometimes speeding and other times slowing down, especially when speaking to the passenger. While driving, they will often face the passenger because of their friendly and conversational nature, which can be frightening to the passenger.

The sanguine loves to shop, overspends for unnecessary items, and is attracted to flashy or colorful objects and advertisements. Bright colors, particularly orange shades ranging from orange-red to orange-yellow, are especially attractive to the sanguine temperament. Their grocery carts are most often overloaded. They tend to delay paying bills and rarely cut down on deficit spending to increase their standard of living.

Generally, sanguines are not good students unless endowed with a high IQ and motivation. They are restless, undisciplined, and find it difficult to concentrate because they have a short attention span. They are usually talented writers, and their handwriting tends to be expressive and flamboyant. Their speaking abilities are generally good and intuitive, with tendencies to exaggerate and boast.

As parents, discipline is usually spontaneous, irrational, loud, and explosive, but brief. Threats of punishment are rarely carried out, because sanguines are not disciplined themselves. Their children learn not to be attentive unless the intensity and duration of the outbursts increases. As a result, children of sanguines tend to be permissive and inconsistent, which could lead to lawlessness as they become older. Favorable features of the sanguine parent are the love and comfort they give their children. They truly enjoy and have fun participating in play and activities with them.

3. The Melancholic Temperament

Strengths

The characteristic strengths of the melancholic temperament are tendencies to be creative, analytical, faithful in friendship, and self-sacrificing.

Of all the temperaments, the melancholic usually exhibits the highest IQ and is the most

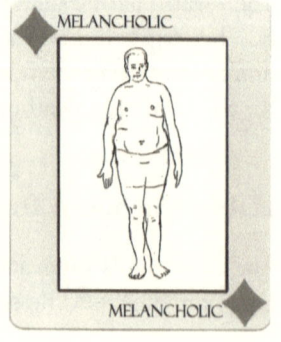

sensitive, creative, and naturally gifted. Melancholics are imaginative, intuitive, and most often perfectionists. They excel in the arts in such fields as painting, sculpting, music, acting, writing, and designing, because they have a vast appreciation for all of life's culture. They tend to be lovers and students of the earth, of gardening, and of animals. The melancholic favors yellow and green, colors of the sun and of plant life.

Melancholics tend to internalize emotional feelings; this influences their thoughts and expressions of creativity. Their tendency toward perfectionism often produces expectations of achievement in others and in themselves that are unrealistic. As a rule, they are self-critical, thinking their earlier performance could have been better, especially in the details. Their analytical and perfectionist tendencies often appear to be critical of new ideas, which they fear may produce future problems.

Melancholics usually do not attract a large number of friends, but they are very faithful to those they do attract. They are likely to be reserved, preferring to be behind the scenes and rarely seeking the limelight. Melancholics seldom volunteer their views or ideas, but when they are asked, they are usually precise and exact based on their analytical reasoning. They are dependable and timely when completing a job because they know their limitations and rarely commit to more than they can handle.

Weaknesses

The main weaknesses of the melancholic center around tendencies to be self-centered, pessimistic, moody, and revengeful. Their tendency to be overly sensitive and self-absorbed can lead to a morbid mental condition. If this condition is not controlled, it could become harmful and destructive to the melancholic's natural and creative strengths. Usually a morose state is brief, but if prolonged, it can be manifested in being too easily offended or insulted, leading to paranoia. The perfectionist and analytical qualities often produce a pessimistic, suspicious, critical, fearful, and indecisive outlook on life. These negative attitudes can outweigh any possible good, as melancholics tend to magnify and fixate their thoughts on possible bad outcomes. This is easily seen in the lack of joy in their lives.

Some melancholics avoid marriage. They desire marriage, but do not marry. They may truly love a potential mate from a distance despite the person's weaknesses, but do not marry as they become aware of these imperfections. Many melancholics believe they are melancholic because they did not marry, not realizing that the reverse is true.

Melancholics generally have greater mood swings than other temperaments. At times, they may be exuberant, but they are more often depressed for no reason. Hippocrates classified them as having "black humors" in their makeup because their depressions are so prominent. Their strong traits of being sensitive, self-centered, and moody can produce long and deep stages of depression. To avoid these tendencies, melancholics often daydream of the "pleasant past" or of a more promising future. They may appear calm or quiet on the surface and yet hide angry, hateful, or resentful feelings. These feelings can occur from minor offenses; incidents that others think are insignificant and should be dismissed easily. If these dangerous thought patterns persist and become severe, a deadening of will and energy could lead to psychotic behavior.

Melancholics are inclined to have their own way and are excessively preoccupied with the faults of others while hiding their own. They frequently exhibit outbursts of excitement, disgust, and bitterness, especially when others are not in agreement with their will and opinions. At the same time, they have difficulty correcting people. They usually show a lack of diplomacy, and are either weak and underreact or outspoken and overreact. In either case, their reproach is generally ineffective and usually offensive. For these reasons, melancholics can harbor a desire for revenge for many years. They may build up so much resentment that they explode in a fit of rage or in a bizarre action that seems unwarranted under the circumstances.

The unforgiving and revengeful weaknesses of this temperament can outweigh the melancholic's brilliant abilities, and could destroy a project, goal, or relationship. There may be little or no reason for this bad outcome other than that the person in charge offended the melancholic in the past. It is paradoxical that the melancholic has the temperament with the greatest strengths and potential, and at the same time possesses the temperament with the greatest weaknesses and self-destructive potential.

Many geniuses and outstanding people in history possess melancholic traits. If the melancholic is dominated by his weaknesses, he may sink below his ability; become a neurotic and hypochondriac person who feels he can no longer enjoy life, and end up wallowing in self-pity.

Habits and Social Traits of the Melancholic

The melancholic is usually on time for appointments, and will likely sigh deeply when arriving with an expression of dejection, self-pity, and unhappiness. Their eating habits are very selective, and they have difficulty deciding what to order. When the food arrives, they relish it all, especially sweets and refined carbohydrates. They prepare well in advance before taking trips or vacations. When driving, they research the best routes extensively and they rarely speed. They generally keep a close account of their traveling expenses.

Melancholics like to shop, but they are cost-conscious and thrifty, comparing prices and quality at different stores before they finally buy. They are knowledgeable about the best buys, coupons, and sale locations.

Melancholics are usually good students with above-average intelligence, and they enjoy learning. They have keen, inquisitive, retentive minds and love books. They are generally good spellers and have an amazing gift of concentration regardless of their disorganized desk, interruptions, or noisy surroundings. Their handwriting is inconsistent and can be illegible, reflecting complexities in themselves.

Melancholics rarely initiate conversations until they have thought out everything beforehand. Once they begin talking, they tend to unleash their entire message. Being perfectionists, melancholics pay bills on time and, although in a disorganized manner, may keep all receipts for several years. They are generally good at bookkeeping and balancing their budgets.

Perfectionist melancholics have unreasonable expectations for their children, who are expected to never do anything less than superior in all school subjects. They usually have rules and procedures for everything and adhere to punishment for offences, although never to excess. They have difficulty in expressing love for their children and do not praise them readily. A melancholic's greatest failing is their habit of bringing up the past failures of family members and close friends.

4. The Phlegmatic Temperament

Strengths

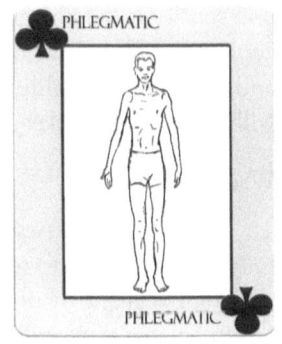

The basic strengths of the phlegmatic temperament are manifested in being witty, dependable, efficient, likeable, and easygoing. Phlegmatics have a naturally dry sense of humor and a superb sense of timing when joking. Their many friends enjoy their slow wit, which is taken from what people say and do. They are good imitators and have retentive minds. They can evoke much laughter from a crowd without cracking a smile. Phlegmatics just say funny things, and, unlike the sanguine, they don't tell a lot of old familiar jokes. Many stand-up comedians have phlegmatic temperaments.

The phlegmatic person has the most well-balanced temperament of all the four. They are dependable, cheerful, and good-natured. They fulfill obligations on time and always do the expected and proper thing. Like the melancholic, they are faithful friends and are rarely disloyal. However, they avoid getting too involved with others. Phlegmatics are basically highly qualified, competent, steady workers who get along well with everyone. They are good listeners who can mediate problems well. They are peacemakers, patient and undemanding. They perform excellently in administration, education, counseling, and any endeavor that requires following orders or giving service to others. Phlegmatics are most often practical, efficient, and well organized in their activities, and appear to have faith in their own abilities. They are not emotionally stimulated to make sudden decisions, but take time to analyze a situation before becoming involved. They want to accomplish an objective with the least amount of time and effort.

Phlegmatics work well under pressure and under circumstances that would be difficult or intolerable for the other temperaments. They are not perfectionists like the melancholic, but they do have a high standard of being correct, accurate, and precise. Phlegmatics are always neat and orderly in the workplace and in the homes. They dress neatly and conservatively, preferring nonprovocative colors, such as blue, gray, and brown. They put things in the same location to avoid spending time and effort looking for them. They don't seek or volunteer for leadership positions; however, if placed in such a position by force or circumstance, they can be very capable and proficient. They manage well and usually have no enemies. They tend to be gentle and humble and do not blame others. They seldom complain about anything.

The phlegmatic is a likeable person and is the greatest friend of all. Everyone considers the phlegmatic a "nice guy." They are easygoing, relaxed, calm, cool, and well-balanced. They are patient, consistent, peaceful, inoffensive, and pleasant. The phlegmatic friend will welcome unexpected visitors and will make time to relax and create conversation.

Weaknesses

The notable weaknesses of the phlegmatic are tendencies to procrastinate or to be slow and lazy, to tease, and to be selfish, stubborn, and indecisive. They are often accused of dragging their feet, and they resent being prodded to action against their will. They don't initiate projects they are qualified to do because it just seems like too much work. They prefer being spectators and are inclined to do as little as possible.

Phlegmatics tend to tease other temperaments that annoy them or threaten to motivate them. They use their wit and humor as a tool to stir up or anger others while they keep their own composure. Phlegmatics tend to be selfish with money, personal effort, and their emotions. They rarely express true feelings of love for another and tend to protect themselves from deep involvement. Phlegmatics are generally stubborn in their views, opposing change, and are naturally conservative, especially with their own time and energy. When asked to do something they don't want to do, they are apt to be quiet, smile, and then not do it. If they are forced into a project that fails, they can be rebellious and more resistant to future suggestions. Their stubborn and selfish tendencies translate to stinginess, especially regarding money matters and avoidance of personal commitment.

The phlegmatic tends to be fearful and indecisive in their desire to please people. Even though they may have a good sense of propriety, they worry for fear of offending someone. They are also indecisive on issues because they often weigh the plan of action against whether they want to expend the time or energy.

Habits and Social Traits of the Phlegmatic

Phlegmatics rarely make appointments, and when they do, they do not readily warm up to discussions and do not enter debates. They generally respond to questions with wit and humor but rarely give opinions unless asked.

They are the most deliberate eaters of all the temperaments and are usually the last to finish eating. This may explain why they rarely gain weight.

The phlegmatic is the slowest driver of all. They tend to stay in the same lane and are hesitant when joining the flow of traffic from an entrance ramp.

They enjoy shopping but are slow, indecisive, and probably more frugal than the other temperaments. They may have to shop more often because of this.

If the phlegmatic can overcome their procrastination tendencies, they can be very good students. They do well with short-term rather than long-term assignments. They work well under pressure and have orderly minds capable of analysis and deductions. They prefer to obtain information from TV rather than from reading materials. Their penmanship is usually small and neat. Phlegmatics almost always systemize their financial records, pay bills on time, and take advantage of discounts for early payments. Balancing their budget is an important event each month.

In raising children, phlegmatics can be good parents but are lax in asserting and confronting unpleasant issues. They love their children, take time with them, play with them, and are patient trainers. Like the melancholic, they may permit their children to sass or intimidate them without showing concern. The phlegmatic parent is the least likely to spank or punish a child, usually leaving that to the more aggressive spouse.

Temperament: Geography, Climate, and the Evolution of Human Beings

This book is not intended to delve into the many theories involving the subjects of geography, climate, and evolution. Suffice it to mention that there appears to be a relationship between temperament and the migration of human beings from their origin. All temperament mixtures exist throughout the world, but a predominance of one temperament type over the others is often highlighted and rationalized in relation to different geographic areas.

The phlegmatic dominant type is often chosen in describing people of the coastal areas of the world, such as England, the Scandinavian countries, and West Africa. The sanguine dominant type is notably found among the people in the inland, hilly, or mountainous countries, such as Ireland, France, Austria, and Italy. The melancholic type often describes the people of the Slav nations, Poland, Russia, and Asia. The choleric dominant type is primarily featured in art and history involving any nation during their periods of power and conquest, such as Greece, the Roman Empire, and France in the era of Napoleon. The choleric physique and temperament is frequently characterized among the Nordic or Germanic people.

It is also reasonable to fathom that in the migration of man, certain geographic climates and areas of the world were preferred and best suited to their genetic predispositions for survival. It would follow that the fair, light-skinned, blue-eyed people fared better in the less sun-intense and colder climate of the northern areas while the darker-skinned, brown-eyed people tolerated and preferred the sun-intense, warmer climate of the areas closer to the equator.

Conclusion

The centuries-old theories of the basic temperaments have been presented, along with many illustrations of how they influence our habits and social traits. In essence, temperaments influence everything in life, including the way we sleep, exercise, decorate, select clothes, and choose hobbies. Our temperament is the answer to the question of why we act and think the way we do.

No one is 100 percent choleric, sanguine, melancholic, or phlegmatic. We are all a genetic combination of the four types. However, the astute person can readily discern the dominant temperament, and in most cases the secondary subdominant temperament, in an individual. In rare cases, only one or up to three temperaments can be identified.

In the next chapter, I will describe the twelve combinations and blends of temperaments that describe the majority of people. This exciting subject is important to understand and to use in our everyday lives. Most people are unaware of the powerful influence temperament has on our behavior. This behavior may not only limit one's potential, but it also affects one's family and all interpersonal relationships. With the discovery of one's basic temperament, one can usually choose what vocational opportunities are most suitable, how to understand and get along with other people, what natural weaknesses to guard against and correct, what type of mate is the most suitable for marriage, and how to make the other important decisions that affect one's life. This knowledge will aid in improving all aspects of life.

In chapter VIII, I will discuss body build and disease predisposition in relation to the basic four temperaments. In the last chapters, suggestions will be made regarding how to modify and balance your temperament for a more harmonious, healthy, and purposeful life.

CHAPTER II

The Twelve Mixtures and Blends of the Temperaments

Prologue

No one represents 100 percent of one temperament, but rather a mixture or blend of the four temperaments. For practical purposes, we will discuss twelve possible blends of the temperaments, in which we consider only one dominant and one secondary (subdominant) temperament. Arbitrarily, the dominant temperament is estimated to be at least 50 percent and the secondary temperament at least 30 percent. In human nature there are varying degrees of temperament within any one blend, so that a ratio of 50 percent to 30 percent sanguine-choleric will be somewhat different than a ratio of 80 percent to 20 percent of the same blend. It is clinically impossible to determine the exact ratios and blends of the four temperaments, as the possibilities of ratios and degrees of blend in human nature would be infinite. Therefore, we are primarily interested in determining the dominant and subdominant temperament in any individual. It is important to realize that a strength in one temperament may cancel out a weakness in another, and vice versa. In about 20 percent of people, the temperament may be so balanced that clinical observation of the dominant and subdominant temperaments is not possible. However, in about 80 percent of the unequal ratios of the temperaments, it is possible to identify rather accurately one of the twelve blends. Considering all of these factors, you will probably still be able to identify yourself and others easier in one of the blends than in one of the basic four temperaments.

DIAGRAM 1
A DIAGRAM OF THE TWELVE BLENDS OF TEMPERAMENTS

	C♠	S♥	M♦	P♣
C♠	~~CC~~	CS	CM	CP
S♥	SC	~~SS~~	SM	SP
M♦	MC	MS	~~MM~~	MP
P♣	PC	PS	PM	~~PP~~

Because no one represents 100 percent of one temperament, the mixtures with the same temperament have been crossed out, producing twelve rather than sixteen blends. While studying the temperament blends, you may think of someone who could fit each blend. That person may be yourself, a friend, a public figure, or a historical figure.

Temperament Mixtures and Blends

1. Choleric-Sanguine (CS)

The choleric-sanguine is the second-strongest extrovert among the blends. Life is completely active for the CS, and his or her efforts are mostly productive and purposeful. CSs are natural communicators, promoters, and salesmen with enough charisma to get along well with all types of people. They are great motivators and thrive on challenges. They appear fearless with boundless energy. As attorneys, they can charm both judge and jury. As fundraisers, they are capable of getting the most tightfisted people to contribute. As preachers, they can inspire their congregations with passion and zeal. As politicians, they can greatly influence their constituents. They are convincing debaters and communicators, although at times they speak with brashness and bravado. In sports and recreation, the CS is fiercely overactive and competitive.

The main weakness of the CS is hostility. They can quickly express explosive anger and resentment. They are impatient with those who do not share their enthusiasm and energy. CSs are very opinionated, prejudiced, impetuous, brutally frank, and hell-bent on completing a project. They don't hesitate to manipulate or walk over other people to accomplish their goal.

Their work takes precedence over family, and the CS will lash out at family members if they complain. Their most prominent weakness is a sharp, fiery, active tongue.

Celebrities Phil Donahue, Arnold Schwarzenegger, Joan Rivers, Judge Judy, and St. Paul appear to fit this blend.

2. Choleric-Melancholic (CM)

The choleric dominant with the subdominant melancholic blend of temperaments produces an extremely industrious, capable person. They overcome the melancholic tendency to be moody by being practical, optimistic, attentive to detail, and goal-oriented. They become exacting leaders with their quick, decisive, and analytical minds. They are extremely competitive, verbally aggressive, and forceful in their actions. CMs are thorough researchers and usually successful in all their pursuits. This temperament generally makes the best natural leader.

Their weaknesses are equally as great as their strengths. They can be authoritative and dictatorial, inspiring both admiration and hate concurrently. Their quick-witted sarcasm can devastate others.

They are natural crusaders and initiators of ideas, who generally harbor hostility and resentment that can cause difficulty in relationships. They tend to be very strict disciplinarians in child rearing, and they combine the hard-to-please nature of the choleric with the perfectionism of the melancholic.

TV personality Bill O'Reilly, General George Patton, Martha Stewart, Ann Coulter, and John F. Kennedy could fit the description of this blend.

3. Choleric-Phlegmatic (CP)

The extroverted trait of the choleric-phlegmatic is less pronounced than in the other choleric-dominant temperaments. The choleric tendency to be quick, decisive, active, and fiery is tempered by the cool, calm, unexcited nature of the phlegmatic. CPs plan in advance and then give great effort to their projects. They prove to be very capable, organized, and deliberate people. They have the ability to bring out the best in other skills. People generally enjoy working with or for the CP. They are likeable, considerate, and not too demanding. The CP generally makes a good spouse and parent. They are excellent in leadership or administrative positions and usually excel in almost any endeavor.

The CP has notable weaknesses, which are mainly harboring resentment and bitterness, although they are not as prone to quick anger as the other choleric blends. Instead of saying cutting or sarcastic remarks, they disguise their sharpness with clever humor. It is at times difficult to determine whether they are kidding or ridiculing. They can be very stubborn once their mind is made up. It is difficult for them to acknowledge a mistake and show regret, but they attempt to make amends subtly. The phlegmatic tendency to worry may curtail the adventuresome spirit of the choleric, and this can thwart their potential.

President Ronald Reagan, John Wayne, Princess Dianna, and Diane Sawyer would tend to represent this temperament blend.

4. Sanguine-Choleric (SC)

The sanguine-choleric represents the strongest extrovert of all the temperaments. Both the sanguine and choleric temperaments that make up their nature are extroverts, and these accentuate each other. The sanguine feature is dominant and is evident in their happy, people-oriented, enthusiastic, salesmanlike qualities. Their less dominant choleric feature influences their behavior to be somewhat more organized and productive than the pure sanguine. They are highly qualified for any position dealing with people, but prefer activity that also offers variety, activity, and excitement.

The notable weakness of the SC is an apparent tendency to be overly extroverted. They usually talk too much and are loud and highly opinionated even before knowing all the facts. At a party, they may be fun and loveable, but if they feel insecure, they can become obnoxious, becoming angry at the slightest provocation. They tend to justify or rationalize their actions—most likely from a weakened conscience resulting from the combined forgetfulness of the sanguine and stubbornness of the choleric. Other weaknesses include being egotistical, weak-willed, and carnal.

Donald Trump, Bette Midler, David Letterman, and Barbara Streisand would be included in this temperament blend.

5. Sanguine-Melancholic (SM)

Sanguine-melancholics are highly emotional people who drastically fluctuate in their moods. They may laugh hysterically one minute and suddenly burst into tears the next minute. Any emotional event, movie, or music can cause them to cry. They genuinely and sincerely relate to the bereavements of others.

SMs possess the qualifications to work in almost any line of work, but are especially gifted in public speaking, acting, music, fine arts, and any creative fields. They are people-oriented and contribute much to the lives of others. However, they must learn to curb the ego and arrogant traits of the sanguine along with the perfectionist, critical nature of the melancholic. These tendencies can obviously alienate and produce hostility in others.

One of the important weaknesses of the SM is their thought pattern. Both the sanguine and the melancholic are dreamers, and if the melancholic part stresses negative thoughts, this can cancel the positive potential. SMs easily develop a poor self-image and have strong tendencies to suffer anger and fear problems, which reflect a deep-seated insecurity. They have a great need to be admired by others, and usually this is a driving force in their performance.

Comedian Don Rickles, King David of the Old Testament, Hillary Clinton, and Madonna could qualify as sanguine-melancholics.

6. Sanguine-Phlegmatic (SP)

The sanguine-phlegmatic is the least extroverted of the sanguine-dominant blends and is the most likely to befriend others. The egotistical outspoken tendencies of a sanguine are cancelled by the gracious, easygoing phlegmatic. They are happy, kind, carefree people with good humor and entertaining qualities that attract people to them. They tend to help others in their work rather than being self-motivated. SPs make their family a priority and treasure the love of their children.

The SP's notable weaknesses are lack of motivation and self-discipline. Socializing and living life casually take priority over working. They are usually optimistic, have an endless repertoire of jokes, and enjoy making people laugh even in the most solemn situations.

Oprah Winfrey, Jay Leno, Andy Rooney of *60 Minutes*, and Goldie Hawn come to mind as having sanguine-phlegmatic temperaments.

7. Melancholic-Choleric (MC)

The melancholic-choleric is both a melancholic perfectionist and a choleric driver. Their melancholic moods are stabilized by their choleric self-will and determination. They are capable of any vocation they seek and possess strong leadership potential. Without fanfare they can excel in any field, whether construction, business, or education. MCs can establish their own career or business and manage it successfully and efficiently. The MC is represented often in orchestras and choral directors.

The outstanding weaknesses of the MC revolve around the natural and compounding weak points of the two basic temperaments, namely, self-persecution, hostility, and criticism. They are difficult to please and rarely express self-satisfaction. Their mood follows their thought process, which is negative for the most part. If such thoughts become persistent, MCs can be intolerable to live with, and they may become manic-depressive. In extreme cases, they can become sadistic and explode in anger. This temperament is not enjoyable company for long periods of time, especially for their spouse and children. They often voice disapproval and may criticize their family verbally for their shortcomings both in public and in private. Because of their spirit of anger, self-persecution, and revenge, they may never live up to their amazing potential.

People who may have MS temperaments could include Napoleon, Mel Gibson, Dr. Laura, and Bill Clinton.

8. Melancholic-Sanguine (MS)

The melancholic-sanguine combines the creative potential of the melancholic with the extroverted qualities of the sanguine. They are usually very gifted and will promote their talents. They can be outstanding musicians, actors, or artists. They are capable of advancing themselves when they are in the right mood. Generally, MSs make excellent teachers. Their melancholic nature will point out interesting trivia and be exacting with details while their sanguine nature generalizes but communicates better with their students.

The main weakness of the MS is big mood swings. When circumstances go their way, they are exceedingly happy, reflecting their sanguine nature. But when things go badly, their dominant melancholic nature can depress them to a deep level of self-pity. In effect, they create their own misery. MSs can be tearful, emotional, rigid, uncooperative, and unreasonably critical of others. Their tendency to be fearful and insecure with a poor self-image often limits them unnecessarily.

Truman Capote, Jonathon Winters, and Roseanne could fit into this temperament blend.

9. Melancholic-Phlegmatic (MP)

The melancholic-phlegmatic is a gifted blend of introverted traits that combine the analytical perfectionist of the melancholic with the organized efficiency of the phlegmatic. They are usually good-natured humanitarians who prefer a quiet, solitary environment for study and research. They are excellent spellers and good mathematicians. Some of the world's greatest scholars who have greatly benefited humanity are MPs, contributing significant inventions and medical discoveries that have advanced civilization.

The MP, like others, also has potential weaknesses. They may become easily discouraged and develop negative thoughts. They can harbor anger and hostility and have a tendency to be vengeful. This temperament blend usually suffers fear, anxiety, and a negative self-image in spite of the fact that they are the people with the greatest talents and capabilities. Commitment to humanitarian causes can trigger them to drain and exhaust their energy and creativity to the point of neglecting their families.

The Apostle John, St. Francis, Albert Einstein, Mother Theresa, and Irving Berlin most likely possessed melancholic-phlegmatic attributes.

10. Phlegmatic-Choleric (PC)

The combined nature of the phlegmatic-choleric features the dominant easygoing traits of the phlegmatic with the less dominant active traits of the choleric. They are easy to get along with and may be excellent group leaders. They are good listeners, interested in people, and can be fine counselors and mediators. PCs are organized, practical, efficient, and trustworthy. Their tendency to be easygoing helps people to relax. People never feel threatened, but instead feel confident when PCs are in control. In their home life, this temperament tends to be passive and reluctant to lead or discipline their children.

The weaknesses of the PC are not readily apparent. They generally lack motivation and harbor an inner fear. They can be stubborn and unyielding in their opinions and actions. If they disagree with others, they never blow up, but quietly maintain their views and won't cooperate. At home, the PC retreats to be alone or nightly immerses his mind watching TV. As they get older, they become increasingly passive and sedentary. Although these tendencies may lead to a long and peaceful life, it can be boring to themselves and their family. They need to be more involved in the concerns and needs of their families.

Frank Sinatra, Gerald Ford, Margaret Thatcher, Condoleezza Rice, and Julia Robertscome are likely phlegmatic-cholerics.

11. Phlegmatic-Sanguine (PS)

The phlegmatic-sanguine combines the best features of both the dominant phlegmatic and the subdominant sanguine temperaments. They are the easiest of all the blends to get along with over a long period of time. The phlegmatic part is evident in their easygoing, congenial, dependable, and witty nature, and the lesser sanguine part provides their happy, people-oriented, and fun-loving nature. They are also thoughtful and diplomatic and seldom display an abrasive personality. They enjoy quiet lives and love their spouses and children. They are usually family oriented and participate in school and church activities.

The weakness of the PS is not pronounced, besides the lack of motivation inherent in the phlegmatic and the lack of discipline of the sanguine. For these reasons, many PSs may not fulfill their true potential. They may not complete their education, they may pass up promising opportunities, and they could avoid anything that requires "too much effort." Inner feelings of fear and insecurity are their self-defeating traits. Depending on the ratio of this temperament blend, PSs may tend to hide in a self-built shell and selfishly avoid activity that would enrich themselves and their families.

TV personalities Andy Griffith, Ray Romano, Carol Burnett, and Paul Seidman appear to fit the characteristics of the phlegmatic-sanguine.

12. Phlegmatic-Melancholic (PM)

The phlegmatic-melancholic is the most gracious, gentle, and quiet blend of all the temperaments. The phlegmatic nature cancels out the negative aspects of the melancholic for the most part. PMs rarely get angry or hostile, and they talk very little. They do the proper thing and tend not to embarrass themselves or others. They dress simply and are dependable, exact, neat, and organized in their work. As a rule, PMs are handy and keep their home in good repair.

Phlegmatic-melancholic weaknesses primarily involve their reluctance to lead or to be aggressive, and their tendency to neglect disciplining their children. They also have weaknesses that involve selfishness, negativism, criticism, and a lack of a positive self-image. Their inner fear and negative feeling of self can prevent them from totally succeeding or getting very involved in anything.

Comedian Don Knotts, Laura Bush, and Jackie Kennedy Onassis represent this temperament blend.

What Is Your Temperament Blend?

Usually it is easier to identify yourself in one of the twelve blends than in the basic four temperaments. Some of you will find it difficult to fit into one of the twelve blends comfortably. No two human beings are alike in all respects, and consequently this is not an exact science, and it may be unsatisfactory to some. But of all behavior theories, the temperament theory has several advantages that make it the most helpful in the majority of cases. In 20 percent or less of instances, there are variables that could cause confusion in arriving at any model that fits precisely. Consider the following factors.

- The percentages of the two blends could vary in extent, to create a much different picture than the 50/30 ratio used here. For example, a ratio of 50/30 sanguine-phlegmatic would be significantly different than a ratio of 80/15 sanguine-phlegmatic.
- Variations in backgrounds, childhood training, and environmental factors could psychologically alter strengths and weaknesses.
- Objectivity could be missing when analyzing yourself. Assistance from someone who knows you well may be necessary.
- Differences in IQ, education, and experience could influence the appraisal of one's temperament.

Generally, in spite of these considerations, the strengths and weaknesses of one's temperament blend do not change.

Health and metabolism can influence temperaments. Examples include hyperthyroid and hypothyroid function, high and low blood pressure, and any form of invalidism or chronic disease.

A small percentage of people may have three relatively close and balanced percentages of temperaments that could make a possible fit, such as 35 percent choleric, 30 percent sanguine, and 30 percent melancholic, with 5 percent phlegmatic.

Masking may influence the outcome of the personality profile test. This is an attempt to conceal one's true temperaments by favoring the traits of another temperament. This is usually done by children to please their parents or by those who think this will improve their acceptance by others.

Motivation, for any reason, can correct an imbalance of behavior. Temperament blend, nevertheless, will always remain.

Self-Analysis

In my own self-analysis, I have discovered that my temperament blend is sanguine-melancholic (SM) with at least 50 percent being sanguine and 35 percent melancholic. The lesser temperaments were 10 percent phlegmatic and 5 percent choleric. As I reviewed the major events of my life, it was interesting to note that at times I gravitated toward the sanguine traits and at other times toward the melancholic traits. In my early teenage period (twelve to sixteen years of age), I had a natural talent and inclination toward music, singing, acting, and comedy. Growing up with the late Don Knotts was a happy period. Together we created and gave performances in our hometown community and rural areas of West Virginia. Those activities, plus playing the tuba in the high school band, strongly revealed my sanguine temperament. The melancholic subdominant feature became prominent in my later teenage period (sixteen to eighteen years of age) when I seriously considered becoming a concert violinist. The love of classical music was a result of pleasant experiences participating in a string quartet and the university symphony by invitation, and giving violin solo performances.

The subdominant melancholic temperament became subdued when I studied medicine and took up the banjo as a hobby and for relaxation. I became seriously interested in playing the banjo after becoming friends with leading banjoists like Eddy Peabody, Eddie Collins, and Father Joseph Dustin, who are all now deceased. Ultimately, I was recognized as an accomplished banjoist and made several recordings. This episode in my life highlighted my dominant sanguine temperament. Now that I am older and more reflective, my melancholic subdominant trait is becoming prominent again. It is revealed in my interest in the meanings of life, wisdom of the ages, spirituality, and writing this book. When I look back, it seems that everything had meaning and purpose to bring me to this point in my life, including past unhappiness, sadness, or suffering that we all experience. All experiences in life, even though we regard them as good or bad, successes or failures, acceptances or rejections, are really great lessons given by some great teachers.

CHAPTER III

A Personality Profile Test

The personality profile test used in my practice for more than ten years was taken from *After Every Wedding Comes a Marriage* by Florence Littauer. It is reproduced here with permission. On my initial consultation with a patient, a preliminary clinical diagnosis of temperament type was indicated on a record of what I considered to be the order of their temperament sequence. Large letters were used for abbreviation, for example, MCSP, indicating that I felt melancholic was the dominant temperament and choleric was the secondary or subdominant temperament. The last two temperaments, sanguine and phlegmatic, were the least prevalent. This determination was made by clinical evaluation of the patient's body build and by observation of body language and reactions to conversation, mainly involving personal interests, hobbies, vocations, medical history, marital status, and children. (Evaluation of physical characteristics in relation to symptoms and disease predisposition will be discussed later.)

With the patients' permission, I would then ask them to complete the personality profile test in order to confirm or negate my clinical impression of the sequence of their temperament dominance. In more than five hundred patients examined, I found that my appraisal of the first two dominant temperaments was correct in approximately 80 percent of the cases. Of these cases, I correctly selected the predominant first and subdominant second temperaments in more than half. In the approximately 20 percent of cases remaining, I could not correctly determine the temperament blend by observation. In most of these instances, the temperaments were almost balanced, and the predominant temperament was not clinically discernable. A few of these indiscernible cases were due to masking, which was discussed in part III. The 80 percent accuracy led me to believe that knowledge of the temperaments would be helpful to anyone interested in identifying their personal temperaments, improving themselves, and understanding and dealing with others.

The personality profile test is an important tool in checking the accuracy of the temperaments you have identified as yours after reading the previous chapters. It gives a fairly accurate picture of the degrees and distribution of the combined four temperaments. It also reveals both the strengths and weaknesses associated with the blend. The general information obtained from the test is of value in understanding yourself and others and how you may respond to various circumstances. The personality profile test is especially useful as an adjunct in determining job skills, interviewing for employment, teamwork adaptability, choosing a mate, parenting, and in all aspects of life requiring proper decisions and communication with others.

To complete the personality profile, answer all forty questions. Transfer your answers to the score sheet and add the totals of both the strengths and weaknesses. You can then easily interpret your dominant personality, and you will know the order of your combination of temperaments.

The knowledge you will gain from the material in this book along with the results of the personality profile test will be valuable in identifying your temperament blend and discovering your strengths and weaknesses. This will be invaluable as you learn to promote your strengths and reduce your weaknesses in order to live a fuller, happier life.

Your Personality Profile

Directions: In each of the following rows of four words across, place an X in front of the one word that most often applies to you. Continue through all forty lines. Be sure each number is marked. If you are not sure which word "most applies," ask your spouse or a friend, and think of what your answer would have been when you were a child.

Strengths

1	___ Adventurous	___ Adaptable	___ Animated	___ Analytical
2	___ Persistent	___ Playful	___ Persuasive	___ Peaceful
3	___ Submissive	___ Self-sacrificing	___ Sociable	___ Strong-willed
4	___ Considerate	___ Controlled	___ Competitive	___ Convincing
5	___ Refreshing	___ Respectful	___ Reserved	___ Resourceful
6	___ Satisfied	___ Sensitive	___ Self-reliant	___ Spirited
7	___ Planner	___ Patient	___ Positive	___ Promoter
8	___ Sure	___ Spontaneous	___ Scheduled	___ Shy
9	___ Orderly	___ Obliging	___ Outspoken	___ Optimistic
10	___ Friendly	___ Faithful	___ Funny	___ Forceful
11	___ Daring	___ Delightful	___ Diplomatic	___ Detailed
12	___ Cheerful	___ Consistent	___ Cultured	___ Confident
13	___ Idealistic	___ Independent	___ Inoffensive	___ Inspiring
14	___ Demonstrative	___ Decisive	___ Dry humor	___ Deep
15	___ Mediator	___ Musical	___ Mover	___ Mixes easily
16	___ Thoughtful	___ Tenacious	___ Talker	___ Tolerant
17	___ Listener	___ Loyal	___ Leader	___ Lively
18	___ Contented	___ Chief	___ Chart maker	___ Cute
19	___ Perfectionist	___ Pleasant	___ Productive	___ Popular
20	___ Bouncy	___ Bold	___ Behaved	___ Balanced

Printed with permission from
After Every Wedding Comes a Marriage by Florence Littauer.

Your Personality Profile

Weaknesses

21 ___ Blank	___ Bashful	___ Brassy	___ Bossy
22 ___ Undisciplined	___ Unsympathetic	___ Unenthusiastic	___ Unforgiving
23 ___ Reticent	___ Resentful	___ Resistant	___ Repetitious
24 ___ Fussy	___ Fearful	___ Forgetful	___ Frank
25 ___ Impatient	___ Insecure	___ Indecisive	___ Interrupts
26 ___ Unpopular	___ Uninvolved	___ Unpredictable	___ Unaffectionate
27 ___ Headstrong	___ Haphazard	___ Hard to please	___ Hesitant
28 ___ Plain	___ Pessimistic	___ Proud	___ Permissive
29 ___ Angered easily	___ Aimless	___ Argumentative	___ Alienated
30 ___ Naïve	___ Negative attitude	___ Nervy	___ Nonchalant
31 ___ Worrier	___ Withdrawn	___ Workaholic	___ Wants credit
32 ___ Too sensitive	___ Tactless	___ Timid	___ Talkative
33 ___ Doubtful	___ Disorganized	___ Domineering	___ Depressed
34 ___ Inconsistent	___ Introvert	___ Intolerant	___ Indifferent
35 ___ Messy	___ Moody	___ Mumbles	___ Manipulative
36 ___ Slow	___ Stubborn	___ Show-off	___ Skeptical
37 ___ Loner	___ Lord over others	___ Lazy	___ Loud
38 ___ Sluggish	___ Suspicious	___ Short-tempered	___ Scatterbrained
39 ___ Revengeful	___ Restless	___ Reluctant	___ Rash
40 ___ Compromising	___ Critical	___ Crafty	___ Changeable

Personality Scoring Sheet

Now transfer all your X's to the corresponding words on this Personality Scoring Sheet and add up your totals. For example, if you checked Animated on the profile, check it on the scoring sheet. (Note: The words are in a different order on the profile and the scoring sheet.)

Strengths

	Popular Sanguine	Powerful Choleric	Perfect Melancholic	Peaceful Phlegmatic
1	Animated	Adventurous	Analytical	Adaptable
2	Playful	Persuasive	Persistent	Peaceful
3	Sociable	Strong-willed	Self-sacrificing	Submissive
4	Convincing	Competitive	Considerate	Controlled
5	Refreshing	Resourceful	Respectful	Reserved
6	Spirited	Self-reliant	Sensitive	Satisfied
7	Promoter	Positive	Planner	Patient
8	Spontaneous	Sure	Scheduled	Shy
9	Optimistic	Outspoken	Orderly	Obliging
10	Funny	Forceful	Faithful	Friendly
11	Delightful	Daring	Detailed	Diplomatic
12	Cheerful	Confident	Cultured	Consistent
13	Inspiring	Independent	Idealistic	Inoffensive
14	Demonstrative	Decisive	Deep	Dry humor
15	Mixes easily	Mover	Musical	Mediator
16	Talker	Tenacious	Thoughtful	Tolerant
17	Lively	Leader	Loyal	Listener
18	Cute	Chief	Chart maker	Contented
19	Popular	Productive	Perfectionist	Pleasant
20	Bouncy	Bold	Behaved	Balanced

Totals—Strengths

☐　　　　☐　　　　☐　　　　☐

Weaknesses

	Popular Sanguine	Powerful Choleric	Perfect Melancholic	Peaceful Phlegmatic
1	___ Brassy	___ Bossy	___ Bashful	___ Blank
2	___ Undisciplined	___ Unsympathetic	___ Unforgiving	___ Unenthusiastic
3	___ Repetitious	___ Resistant	___ Resentful	___ Reticent
4	___ Forgetful	___ Frank	___ Fussy	___ Fearful
5	___ Interrupts	___ Impatient	___ Insecure	___ Indecisive
6	___ Unpredictable	___ Unaffectionate	___ Unpopular	___ Uninvolved
7	___ Haphazard	___ Headstrong	___ Hard to please	___ Hesitant
8	___ Permissive	___ Proud	___ Pessimistic	___ Plain
9	___ Angered easily	___ Argumentative	___ Alienated	___ Aimless
10	___ Naïve	___ Nervy	___ Negative attitude	___ Nonchalant
11	___ Wants credit	___ Workaholic	___ Withdrawn	___ Worrier
12	___ Talkative	___ Tactless	___ Too sensitive	___ Timid
13	___ Disorganized	___ Domineering	___ Depressed	___ Doubtful
14	___ Inconsistent	___ Intolerant	___ Introvert	___ Indifferent
15	___ Messy	___ Manipulative	___ Moody	___ Mumbles
16	___ Show-off	___ Stubborn	___ Skeptical	___ Slow
17	___ Loud	___ Lord over others	___ Loner	___ Lazy
18	___ Scatterbrained	___ Short-tempered	___ Suspicious	___ Sluggish
19	___ Restless	___ Rash	___ Revengeful	___ Reluctant
20	___ Changeable	___ Crafty	___ Critical	___ Compromising

Totals—Weaknesses

☐　　　　☐　　　　☐　　　　☐

Combined Totals

☐　　　　☐　　　　☐　　　　☐

CHAPTER IV

The Four Body Types and Body Blends (Physiques)

The studies of body physique by W. H. Sheldon in his book *The Varieties of Human Physique* involved the study of four thousand students of Swabian descent. He closely observed the young men, and then divided the different physiques into three primary types and associated each of these types with one of the three human primordial layers of the embryonic disc—namely, ectoderm or outer layer, mesoderm or middle layer, and endoderm or inner layer. The ectoderm (outer layer) changed into skin, hair, nails, and the central nervous system. The mesoderm (middle layer) changed into muscle, bone, the vascular system, the connective tissues, and the stroma of the internal organs. The endoderm (inner layer) changed into all the linings of the inner body, primarily the respiratory and gastrointestinal systems. The physique in which one of the areas predominated was named accordingly—ectomorph (body where ectodermal features predominate), mesomorph (body where mesoderm features predominate), and endomorph (body where endoderm features predominate).

Sheldon described the three types in their extreme characteristics. He realized that the mixtures and gradations of the three types are infinite and that the relative frequency of a blend could result in a fourth body type that is between the mesomorph and endomorph. The high frequency of occurrence of people that fit the characteristics of a mixture between mesomorph and endomorph became the fourth temperament designated "sanguine." The mesomorph corresponds to the choleric temperament, and the endomorph corresponds to the melancholic type. The phlegmatic temperament represents the ectomorphic type. Any system considered a scientific classification of all different body types and mixture does not lend itself to any degree of accuracy. However, Sheldon used measurements of all parts of the basic body types and took photographs to verify that the varieties of the mixtures increase at the midpoint of all of the body types (see Chart 5).

In a series of four thousand individuals with reference to all of the physical characteristics, Sheldon found that the absolute pure variant does not exist. Though many physiques showed a strong predominant trend toward one of the polar extremes, each body also exhibited minor local characteristics belonging to one of the other types.

Chart 3 illustrates the fundamental four body types. Chart 4 depicts the relative differences in the predominant facial expressions, hand size, and side portraits of the four dominant temperaments. These charts can be a helpful reference while reading the description of each basic body type.

Chart 3

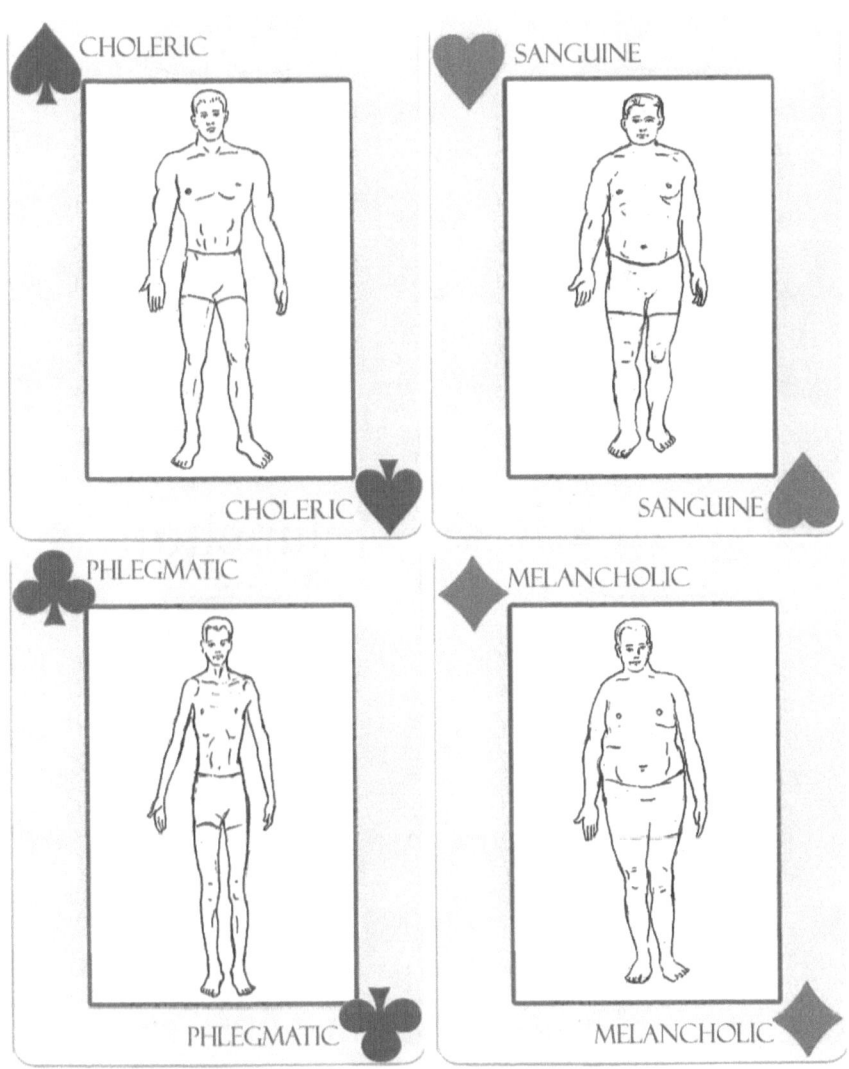

Diagrams by Virginia Ferrara Twaits

Chart 4

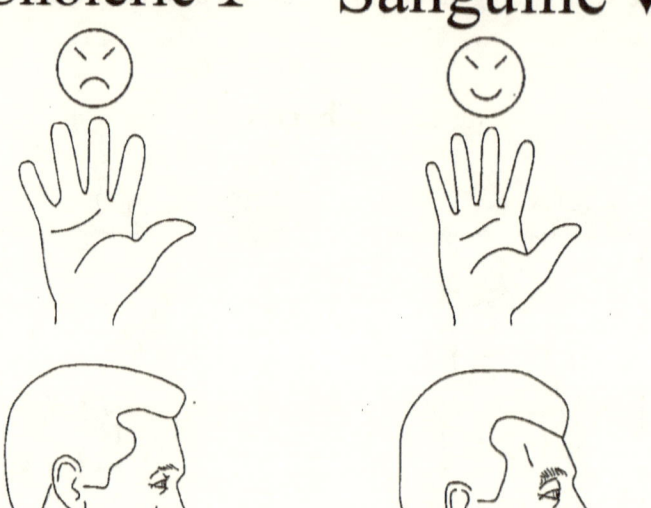

Choleric ♠   Sanguine ♥

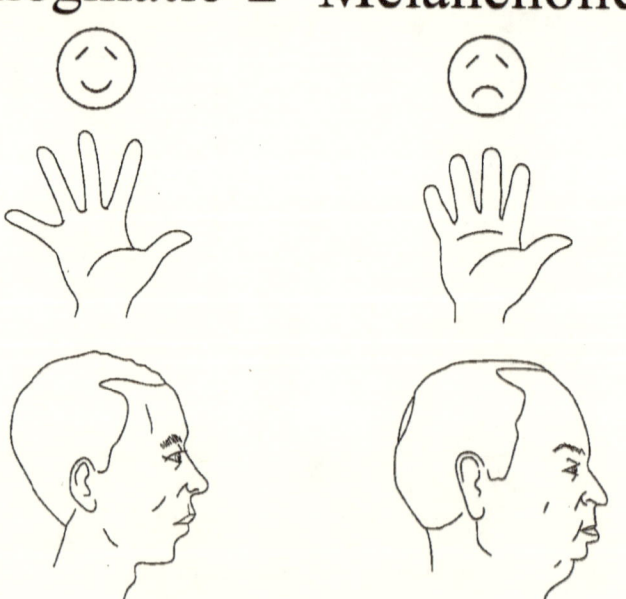

Phlegmatic ♣ Melancholic ♦

Drawing by Virginia Ferrara Twaits

A circular diagram with the examples of the four body types equally distributed (Chart 5) simplifies Sheldon's classification and statistics, which are based on the ratio of frequencies of the body blends. Because of the high incidence of mixture between choleric and melancholic, there appears to be the fourth body type that he suggested, which would nicely describe the sanguine body build. The direction of the black full arrows indicate the predominant body type. The numbers indicate relative occurrences of the body types and blends (taken from analysis of four thousand males by W. H. Sheldon, PhD, MD). The capital letters (i.e., CS) represent the first letter of the dominant and secondary temperament blend.

Chart 5

DIAGRAM OF THE FOUR BODY TYPES AND POSSIBLE BODY BLENDS

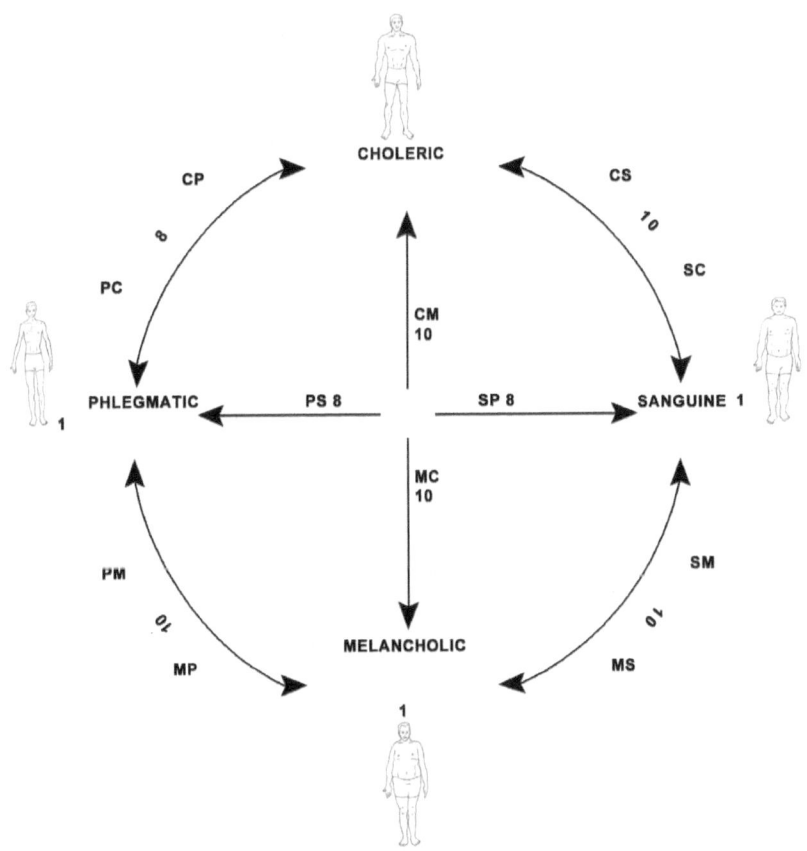

In my practice I adhered to the physical characteristics of the various body types as described primarily by Sheldon. They were in general agreement with my clinical observations.

The predominant body type generally correlates with the predominant personality temperament in the majority of cases. However, in approximately 20 percent of undetermined cases, there may be individuals who possess a personality temperament with a clinically different body type. These are referred to in the literature as dysplastic types, and they can be substantiated by psychological testing. The physical characteristics used in determining body type can be complex when one considers age, weight, sex, height, race, health status, nutrition, occupation, environment, and the possibility of dysplasia. However, a keen and practiced observer of human nature can, in the majority of cases, correctly assess and correlate the predominant body type with the associated personality temperament.

It is important to note that the characteristics of the four body types described in the following sections represent extreme examples. The descriptions of the various parts of the body are in the same order within each example. A general characterization of each body type precedes the more detailed and specific local description of body parts.

The male physique is primarily featured because the physical traits of their body types and blends are more prominent and easier to discern than in the female physique. Physical traits in the female, however, are similar but less evident.

The Choleric Physique

The choleric-dominant physique is characterized by the pronounced development of the bony skeleton, the general musculature, and the skin.

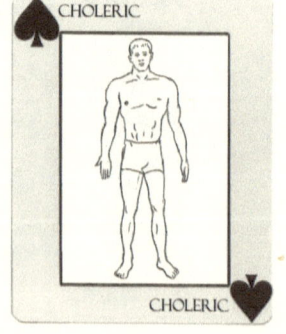

A general description entails a midsized to tall person with particularly wide projecting shoulders, a well-developed chest, a firm abdomen, and a trunk that tapers in the lower regions. The pelvis and muscular legs blend gracefully when compared with the large upper limbs and projecting shoulders.

The long solid head is carried upright on a full neck that has a sloping contour of the firm trapezius muscle on either side of the neck. The shape of the head and face is most often elongated or egg shaped, giving the impression of a larger forehead. The chin is usually long and sometimes cone shaped. The choleric head is frequently rectangular, square, or shield shaped, giving a hard appearance. The strong, bony structure of the face gives it a plastic appearance with prominent supraorbital arches (brow ridge), compact cheekbones, and a heavy and strong-looking. The occipital prominence at the base of the skull is generally well developed. The skin over the face and body appears thick, firm, and elastic. The subcutaneous fat is only moderately developed and appears more or less normal. The overdeveloped musculature throughout the body stands out through a very thin sheath of fat.

The skin of the face usually reveals large visible pores with a tendency to acne, and can be pasty and sometimes puffy in appearance. There may be a dark reddening of the face behind an otherwise pale complexion. The eyes give the impression of a glint in the eagle-like expression, which is firm, energetic, and fiery.

The scalp hair is generally coarse and abundant and tends to encroach on the forehead from the sides of the temple areas. Baldness is variable and usually appears on the frontal area and tends to be patchy over the scalp. The body hair is also coarse and hairiness (hirsutism) is variable. There is usually a masculine distribution of hair about the lower abdomen, pubic area, and groin that takes on a diamond-shaped configuration.

The extremities are remarkable in their development. They are heavily muscled, especially the forearms and calves. The length of the extremities is generally longer than in the other types. The upper extremity reaches to or below the midthigh level, which affords the choleric more power and endurance. The hands and wrists are commonly larger, with greater circumferences than in the other types. The shape of the hands tends to correspond to the shape of the head and face. When the face is rectangular or shield shaped, the palms are commonly rectangular, and the fingers are thick and square ended. The toes are of a similar configuration. The height of the choleric may vary, but generally they are taller than the other temperaments. They walk with a firm, almost hurried step. The chest is full, well tapered, and muscular. The trunk as a whole has a relatively flat appearance and is long with a low lumbar curve (in the lower back). The waist and abdomen tend to be firm and muscular, and appear fairly narrow because of the massive muscles of the pelvic girdle and a roll of muscle over the iliac crests. The genitalia are almost always well developed, in the male, compact with a firm thick scrotum.

The choleric woman corresponds to the male form with certain deviations. The fat development may be more prominent, but in good proportion to the rest of the body. Female cholerics generally give the impression of overdevelopment, solidity, and massiveness, and may impart a more masculine appearance. The elongated egg-shaped face is more common than a larger wide face and prominent cheekbones.

The choleric physique may be realized at an early age, but often becomes apparent by puberty. It reaches full development after twenty-five years of age. The physique usually stays the same, with little or no tendency toward weight gain or obesity throughout life. In old age, the musculature may atrophy or degenerate, most likely due to endogenous factors and inactivity.

The Sanguine Physique

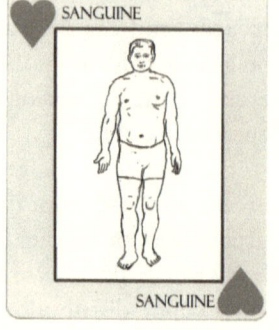

The sanguine-dominant physique is characterized by the pronounced development of the head, chest, and abdomen. There is a greater tendency toward distribution of fat around the trunk. The shoulders and extremities are less pronounced in fat distribution.

A general description entails a middle-sized person of average height, usually shorter than the choleric, with a rounded applelike figure, a soft broad face, and a short massive neck sitting between the shoulders. Obesity in the sanguine is usually moderate, primarily involving the trunk. More often than not, the sanguine tends to wear a belt below the protruding upper abdomen. The hips and buttocks are generally inconspicuous, narrow, and flat.

The typical sanguine face is a true mirror of the sanguine physique. The face tends to be hexagonal in shape, wide, soft, and round in appearance. The middle segment of the face (nose and cheeks) predominates. The eyes tend to be large and convey a cheerful and friendly spirit. The skin of the cheeks and nose reveals a tendency toward blushing and redness, and the presence of superficial blood vessels are frequently visible. This feature indicates a hypersensitivity of the vasomotor system and a predisposition to acne rosacea.

The head in general is large, wide, round, and deep, although not very high. It sinks forward between the shoulders, so that the short thick neck seems to disappear and the upper back takes on a bend or hunch. Fine thinning of the scalp or baldness, when present, generally involves both the front and top of the scalp while sparing the sides.

Sheldon's studies of scalp and body hair suggest a tendency for abundance of hair and hirsutism in the sanguine associated more with choleric predominance than with melancholic predominance. The skin over the face and body is smooth, well fitting, and of moderate thickness. Compared to the choleric, the sanguine has relatively short extremities and a longer trunk. When extended, the upper extremities reach above midthigh. The shoulders are not broad and projecting as with the choleric, but are rounded rather high and pushed forward together, giving a characteristically sharp depression on the inner deltoid curve. The extremities tend to be soft and rounded with little evidence of muscle or bone prominence. However, some sanguine people may have solid, heavy bodies with great strength and energy. The hands are usually soft, plump, and rather short and wide. The joints of the hand are often slim and elegantly formed. The gait of the sanguine is usually quick, light-footed, and dancelike. The thorax appears wide, deep, and longer than the extremities. The genitalia vary in development, being larger and stronger when choleric predominates, and smaller and weaker when melancholic predominates.

In sanguine women, the fat distribution around the trunk is more concentrated over the breasts and hips. When the choleric predominates, the breasts are not as large, and the hips, buttocks, and extremities are fuller, with more fat distribution.

The younger sanguine can easily be confused with the choleric at first sight, but with careful observation, the ratio between shoulder width and chest width will reveal the difference. The sanguine is below the choleric in shoulder width but above him in chest width and measurement. The deltoid depression is also usually present in young sanguines.

Weight changes in the sanguine can be abrupt, especially in connection with certain periods of life. From about thirty years of age, a rapid increase in weight frequently occurs until middle age, most often with numerous vacillations. After age sixty, consistent with psychological depression, the weight may fall rapidly and remain low even when the depression is removed. In older sanguines, the buttocks are flat, and legs can be surprisingly thin.

The Melancholic Physique

The melancholic-dominant physique is characterized by a large head and a triangular-shaped face, a round, hourglass trunk, high waist and high hips, a fat roll above the pubic area, and "ham" formation of the upper arms and legs. More often than not, the bony structure and muscles are weak.

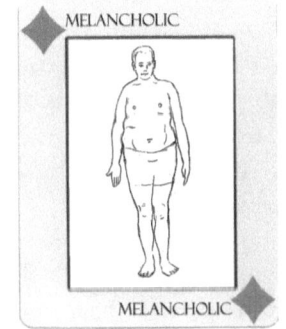

An average-sized melancholic has a large, round upper head and face that tapers down to a smaller lower face and weak chin, imparting a triangular form. Facial features are soft and well related, often with a shapeless mouth, flabby lips, and sleepy eyes. An interesting point in diagnosis is the oral examination of the hard palate. In the melancholic, the hard palate is wide, low, and parabolic, whereas in the phlegmatic, the hard palate is high and narrow. The neck is likely to be longer and thinner than in the sanguine, with no evidence of muscularity. The angle between the jaw and neck is partially erased by fat accumulation. When the chin is sharply receding, this angle disappears altogether.

The skin of the face and body is soft, smooth, and velvety. The eyes look more or less sad, sleepy, and troubled. Hair on the scalp and body tends to be fine and not particularly hirsute. Often, however, hair is seen over the breasts and the upper back, and sometimes over the shoulders. Baldness may be premature and is seen as a round area beginning at the top of a broadly domed head and gradually spreading peripherally in almost a perfect circle, leaving a polished surface with a fine hair texture. Pubic hair takes on a triangular feminine-type distribution.

The extremities are characterized by having a "ham" shape of the upper arms and thighs. Both upper and lower extremities are long in relation to the trunk, and the arm span reaches to the upper thighs. The forearms are invariably slender, but the lower legs may vary from frail and stilt-like to fat shapeless forms. There is a strong tendency to develop "knock knees" and occasionally pigeon-toe feet. This temperament cannot easily bring their heels together when standing. Their gait is usually slow and heavy.

The hands correspond with the form of the face and head. The shape of the hand is generally long and triangular, and the fingers are long. The feet mimic the hand formation. The height may vary widely, but they are almost always shorter than the choleric.

The upper chest tends to show some flattening in front, but, as a whole, is round. The shoulders are narrow and nonprojecting, the widest point of the chest falls about the level of the nipples, and the breast formation is distinct. The waist, hips, and buttocks are extremely high and prominent.

The lower abdomen is wide, deep, and protuberant, imparting a pear shape to the body. They will usually wear their belts midabdomen above a notable roll of fat above the pubic area. The mass of the abdomen considerably exceeds the mass of the chest. A marked characteristic is that the widest part of the body most often falls below the waist and well above the iliac crests (hip bone) instead of over the trochanters (hip joints) as in the other temperament types.

The curves of the body plus the secondary hair distribution impart a feminine suggestion. The spine is often collapsed, with a sharp lumbar lordosis (forward bend), giving the body a shorter look. A compensating high kyphosis (hump of the upper back) causes the neck to project forward. The genitalia are most often hypoplastic or underdeveloped, but this may vary depending on the secondary temperament type.

Melancholic women are very similar in characteristics to the melancholic men except for being smaller in stature.

Age accentuates the lumbar lordosis, and melancholics may become shorter and frailer. Senile skin changes are moderate and not as pronounced as in the phlegmatic.

The Phlegmatic Physique

The phlegmatic-dominant physique is character-ized by a general diminished development of all parts of the body, face, neck, trunk, and extremi-ties, and in all the tissues—skin, fat, muscle, bone, and vascular system. The decreased image portrays linearity, fragility, delicate constitution, small frail bones, and thready muscles. This is evident in both phlegmatic males and females.

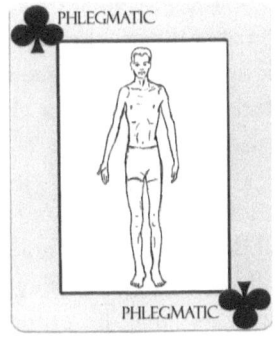

The phlegmatic male is a lean, narrowly built man, usually of average height but weighing less than the average male. He appears taller than he is, with pale, dry skin. He exhibits narrow shoulders, long lean extremities, and a flat chest with evident bony ribs. A sharp rib angle and a thin abdomen give the appearance of being long and narrow, sallow, thin, and sharply molded.

The head, compared with the other temperament types, is generally short and somewhat narrow, and the back of the head is steep with little roundness. The top of the head is often flat. The well-marked cheekbones and the brow ridge are due to the overlying transparent and thin skin and not to strong bony growth. One important characteristic is the disproportion between the great length of the nose and the short, small chin and lower jaw. From a side view, the forehead slopes forward along the bridge of the nose to its tip, and from there the profile goes straight back to the short little chin. A common feature is the presence of coursing dilated blood vessels at the sides of the temples. The front view usually manifests a shortened egg-shaped face, and the lower jaw runs downward from the ears to the tip of the chin. The eyes appear faint and devoid of expression. The neck is long with a gooseneck ap-pearance, frequently with a protruding Adam's apple or sloping neckline.

The skin is generally thin, lacking in fat, flabby, nonelastic, dry, and pale in color. The diminished elasticity is evidenced by the skin returning slowly to its original position after being pinched. The skin often shows fine wrinkling on exposed surfaces. History reveals that the skin does not tan well, burns eas-ily, peels quickly, and returns to the pale color. The phlegmatic has difficulty maintaining an even temperature; this is apparently related to the relatively greater body surface. They do not tolerate extremes in heat or cold well.

Scalp hair is fine and grows rapidly; phlegmatics rarely become bald. The secondary body hair and pubic hair are variable, but are most often fine and sparse. The upper and lower extremities are equally lean with thin muscles. The thighs and upper arms are notably weak. The extremities are longer than the trunk and very flexible. The arms may reach to midthigh. The lower extremities are separated by a gap between the thighs.

The phlegmatic's gait tends to be lazy and sluggish; however, some are great walkers. The hands and feet are delicate and narrow. The fingers are long, bony, and frequently loose or double-jointed. The hands and feet may feel cold and have a chronic cyanotic appearance of a blue-red color that blanches on pressure.

Phlegmatics have a trunk that is relatively short and limbs that are relatively long, but they may not be tall. The thorax is long compared with the abdomen. It is flat and receding from the nipple to the clavicle. It is usually narrow and lacking in muscular relief. The lumbar lordosis and thoracic kyphosis may be pronounced. The rounded shoulders droop forward and produce a marked clavicular hollow, which is a characteristic feature of the phlegmatic. The arms seem to hang in front of the body, and the shoulder blades tend to wing out.

The abdomen is flat, relatively short or shallow in depth, and, generally, protrudes out below the navel. The male genitalia usually exhibit marked linearity and hypertrophy as evidenced by a long penis and scrotum.

Phlegmatic women are very similar to phlegmatic men in body characteristics. They are not only thin, but most often of very small stature.

All the phlegmatic characteristics stay constant throughout life. In childhood, phlegmatics may appear weak and frail. In puberty, there is a rapid growth in height and the development of the narrow form. In adulthood and old age, in spite of physical activity or increased food consumption, there is little or no increase in muscle or fat. The face becomes thinner with age and usually shows evidence of premature aging. Even between the ages of thirty-five and forty, there may be senile changes with some wrinkled laxity in the skin and visible protruding veins on the temples. The skin becomes progressively dryer, with some scaling.

CHAPTER V

Constitutional Temperament

Association of Body Type (Physique) and Temperament (Personality)

Throughout the ages, many scholars, writers, and artists have asserted that the shape of a man was associated with certain traits in his temperament. This is evident in the portrayal of characters like witches, devils, jolly fat men, heroes, saints, and religious statues. Hippocrates observed that personality was largely dependent on morphology (body build). As discussed in the chapter I, he established different types of individuals by observation and implication, not by argument or statistical studies. He suggested that those who closely examine people can see a definite correlation between traits of character and body structure. Moreover, many students of the temperament theory have claimed that body structure and temperament are clearly two aspects of the same organism. It is astonishing that this relationship has not been studied more extensively, given that the implications are vital to a person's health. Apparently, this subject matter has so many potential and perplexing variables that a search for the basic factors is daunting. Most of the past literature on this subject has been discarded or ignored because of the confusing and complicated statistics. However, as a rule, the general truth can be simplified and need not be complicated.

Certainly there are exceptions to every rule and observation. As my anatomy professor once said, "There is no such thing as *always* or *never* in nature." When pure clinical observations reveal apparent truths in the majority of cases, then this knowledge should be passed on for future research and study. When this doesn't happen, important knowledge and analysis is lost.

In his book *Transformed Temperaments*, Tim LaHaye related that the study of human nature received a new impetus with the birth of the science of psychology near the end of the nineteenth century. In this book, he discussed the research of Dr. H. Wundt. As mentioned in chapter I, Dr. Wundt performed exhaustive studies trying to relate the four temperaments to body structure in 1879 at Leipzig University. His concept did not take hold, but it did lead to the concept of constitutional temperament, which attributes man's behavioral traits to his body structure.

Sigmund Freud popularized his theory of psychoanalysis, which maintained that man's environment determined his behavior, in the early part of the twentieth century. This concept effectively discredited the temperament theory that man inherits certain personality traits at birth that, though modified by environment to a certain extent, will be evident throughout life. In more recent years, the trend is turning away from Freudian thought. Many modern psychiatrists and psychologists are disenchanted with Freudian ideas and are becoming more interested in other theories that emphasize each person's responsibility for his or her own behavior. The concept is well-documented in the temperament theory and is contrary to the psychoanalytic approach. Effective therapy can be more readily obtained by understanding one's own temperament and balancing out one's strengths and weaknesses with a more holistic approach involving body, mind, and spirit.

Much of the present-day knowledge of physique and the associated personality traits resulted from the extensive investigative work of Dr. William H. Sheldon. An American medical doctor and psychologist, he devoted his professional life to observing the range of human body types and the associated personality traits. He wrote several books on this topic, notably *The Varieties of Human Physique* and *The Varieties of Temperament.* For his study of human physique, he meticulously examined and photographed some four thousand unclothed college-aged men. He discovered that there were three fundamental body types that, when combined together, made up all the various body forms. As mentioned earlier, he named these types endomorph, mesomorph, and ectomorph because they seemed to be derived from the three layers of the human embryo (endoderm, mesoderm, and ectoderm). He further conducted a large number of surveys to investigate whether there was any identifiable connection between physique and temperament type. He concluded that there was a strong correlation, as he had thought. He associated three fundamental types of temperament that he discerned in this survey with the three fundamental body types he had named in his study. He named them in harmony with the morphologic nomenclature, thus, the endotonic personality was associated with the endomorph body type, the mesotonic personality was associated with the mesomorph body type, and the ectotonic personality was associated with the ectomorph body type. Sheldon devised a way of numerically rating the strength of each area based on a checklist of sixty characteristics that describe the basic components. The 7-1-1 was the extreme endomorph and endotonic, the 1-7-1 was the extreme mesomorph and mesotonic, and the 1-1-7 was the extreme ectomorph and ectotonic. There existed a large number of men in the study who rated between the extreme mesomorph and endomorph, which Sheldon admitted could be a fourth body type. (This same fourth body type is described in the original Hippocratic temperament theory as sanguine.) Thus, we have the four body types of the temperament theory, which correspond to the complete description of the body type and their associated temperament. The choleric is Sheldon's mesomorph and mesotonic. The sanguine represents the combination of mesomorph and endomorph. The melancholic represents the endomorph and endotonic, and the phlegmatic represents the ectomorph and ectotonic. Sheldon laboriously studied the personality traits of each body type; these are now documented and expanded to encompass the full spectrum of personality traits as we know them today. He noted several important points regarding the character and physiology of each temperament that are described in the remainder of this chapter.

Cholerics (mesomorphs), with their heavily endowed muscular system, express their basic nature with action and excessive energy. They require less sleep, are ready to go early, and can be active for long periods without rest. They have insensitivity to pain and great endurance, and are generally fearless. They reveal a higher basal metabolism, a higher pulse rate, and a higher blood pressure than average. Their voices tend to be loud and projecting.

The melancholic (endomorph) is not only slower in movement and speech than average, but all their reactions are at a slower rate. This includes the basal metabolism, pulse rate, and breathing rate. Sheldon also noted that the circulation in the hands and feet tend to be poor in people with this temperament.

Dr. Sheldon documented the phlegmatic (ectomorph) character and physiology most thoroughly, and this deserves a detailed review. The phlegmatic loves and seeks privacy and shelter from excessive stimulation, especially when troubled. Because they are so sensitive to outside stimulation, they tend to develop strategies to avoid and/or decrease outside stimulation. They will often cross their legs and curl up in an attempt to minimize their exposure to the external world. More often than not, phlegmatics try to avoid noisy environments and large groups of people. They prefer small groups in protective places. Phlegmatics usually experience sudden hunger, which they must quickly satisfy. They prefer a high-protein, high-calorie diet with frequent snacking, seemingly to accommodate their small digestive system. Also, they may frequently complain of a nervous stomach and nervous or spastic bowel. Their sleep pattern is usually quiet and light with frequent episodes of insomnia. They generally sleep on one side with their legs drawn up in the fetal position. Phlegmatics frequently complain of chronic fatigue and tend to avoid vigorous exercise or physical activity. Their blood pressure is generally low and their pulse weak and fast. Their respirations are shallow and rapid. Their temperature tends to be slightly elevated and promptly rises at the onset of illness. Phlegmatics are notoriously resistant to many major diseases but suffer excessively from insect bites and various skin afflictions. Hypersensitivity to infections can lead to quick physical reactions that can cause incapacitation, such as acute streptococcal throat infection. This condition can adversely progress quickly to produce a marked throat swelling with difficult breathing and swallowing.

Phlegmatics are well aware of their strong feelings, although they do not display them, and consequently people tend to believe they are apathetic and have no feelings. In social situations, they are usually uncomfortable with initial introductions, especially when they have no intimate acquaintances present. Phlegmatics have a lower threshold of pain and are hypersensitive to anticipated pain. Their voices, unlike those of cholerics, are projected only to reach the person they are addressing. The phlegmatic often wears an alert, intent expression and appears younger in public. They mature late in adolescence, and, being future-oriented, consider the latter part of life to be the best years.

The sanguine represents a vast group of people that combine the aspects of the choleric and the melancholic. The perfect sanguine, which is exactly midpoint between the choleric and melancholic, is rare. The usual combination favors either the choleric or the melancholic as the primary dominant. The medical profession is recognizing the sanguine physiology according to which of the two temperaments is more dominant. The sanguines who favor the choleric primary dominant are big-chested, having a heavy upper body, with the abdomen generally protruding above the belt line. They have a tendency to be overweight or obese and are considered apple shaped. They often reveal hyper-insulinism, an elevated fasting blood sugar, a predisposition to diabetes, and a higher blood uric acid. They frequently reveal hypertension and are considered at high risk for cardiovascular complications. Sanguines are warm physically and personally. Their hands, feet, and body radiate heat, and sanguines notably have a strong, firm, and warm handshake. The sanguine that favors the melancholic dominant will reveal physical, personality, and metabolic tendencies of the melancholic temperament. Depending on the degree of melancholia, we would expect a tendency toward lower body obesity, often considered the pear-shaped configuration. The belt is worn high-waisted with the obvious lower abdomen and hip fat protruding. They usually have lower blood pressure, a lower pulse rate, and a lower metabolic rate than the sanguine with choleric dominance. They may exhibit a greater tendency to diabetes, lower thyroid function, and a lower basal metabolic rate. Their hands and feet are not as warm, and cardiovascular disease is not as frequent for them as with the choleric-dominant sanguine. This whole complex of the sanguine temperament has been recently described in the medical literature as Metabolic Syndrome, which includes many more metabolic dysfunctions in addition to the above features. It appears that the recognition of the primary and secondary dominant of the temperament may be of value in future medical research involving physique, temperament, and predisposition to disease.

A Summary of Each Temperament

Chart 6 summarizes the main features of each temperament. It includes a diagram of each body type, temperament traits (strengths and weaknesses), main social features, favorite periods of life, best careers to pursue, personal needs, a personality type, most productive time of day, and their outstanding gift.

Important Features of the Four Temperaments

	Choleric ♣	Sanguine ♥	Melancholic ♦	Phlegmatic ♠
Body Type				
Diagram				
Temperament Traits	**Strengths** Strong Willed, Self Disciplined, Self Confident, Practical, Optimistic, Leader, Aggressive, Decisive — **Weaknesses** Domineering, Angry Cruel, Self-Sufficient, Crafty, Sarcastic, Inconsiderate, Unemotional, Proud	**Strengths** Joy, Love, Warm, Friendly, Out-going, Compassionate, Talkative, Enthusiastic, Care free — **Weaknesses** Weak-willed, Undisciplined, Unstable, Restless, Egocentric, Exaggerates, Fearful, Undependable	**Strengths** Gifted, Analytical, Sensitive, Perfectionist, Idealistic, Aesthetic, Faithful, Self-Sacrificing — **Weaknesses** Rigid, Unsociable, Self-centered, Critical, Moody, Impractical, Revengeful, Negative	**Strengths** Gentle, Calm, Easy Going, Dependable, Efficient, Conservative, Diplomat, Humorous — **Weaknesses** Stingy, Fearful, Indecisive, Selfish, Spectator, Self-Protective, Unmotivated, Weak-Libido
Main Features	Physical Activity, Adventure, Competitive	Socializing, Eating, Relaxing	Creative, Sensitive, Meditative	Solitude, Privacy, Play
Favorite Period of Life	Young Adulthood	Teenage	Childhood	Late Adulthood
Best Careers	Producer, Builder, Leader	Actors, Speakers, Sales Person	Artists, Musical, Philosopher, Professor	Diplomat, Accountant, Teacher, Technician
Needs	Exercise, Action, Expansive Places	People, Fellowship, Mingling	Artistic, Philosophy, Influence	Quiet Protective Places, Introspection, Fantasy
Jungian	Extrovert — Type A	Extrovert — Type A	Introvert — Type B	Introvert — Type B
Most Productive Time	Morning	Evening	Two Hour Cycles	Daytime
Main Gift	Leadership	Communication	Creativity	Loyalty

Chart 6

CHAPTER VI

Diet, Physiology, and Traits of the Temperaments

Preferred Foods and Correlation to Card Suits

Diet and nutrition have become increasingly popular in health-related publications. There is no question that with the advent of technology and the scientific revolution in the manufacture of nutrients, foods produced in the dairy and agriculture industries have supplanted the whole, natural, unaltered foods needed for the maintenance of personal health. The fast food industry has targeted the inherent weakness of human nature by promoting craved foods that will, in excess, unfavorably affect health. Although people are living longer, the incidence of chronic conditions such as obesity, diabetes, hypertension, and cardiovascular diseases are increasing at an alarming rate. The general public is either ignorant of or chooses to ignore the importance of a proper, nutritional, balanced diet to maintain good health. Knowledge of temperaments will reveal that each temperament differs in their preferred foods, flavors, and drinks. Instinctual factors are also involved that relate to constitutional temperament and ancestral inherent traits.

In his book on folk medicine, Dr. D. C. Jarvis, MD, stresses the importance of following natural inherent and ancestral traits in food preference. Randy Rolfe, JD, MA, in her book *The Four Temperaments*, discusses the natural food preferences of different temperaments, but also warns that prolonged overindulgence in favorite foods could lead to a severe humoral imbalance and disease promotion.

Rolfe, in her book on the four temperaments, relates the four suits of a deck of cards with the four temperaments: spades for choleric (C), hearts for sanguine (S), diamonds for melancholic (M), and clubs for phlegmatic (P).

Many investigators of Hippocrates' theory have associated the humors with the symbols of the suits of playing cards. The history and origin of our fifty-two playing cards is cloudy, but appears to be related to the tarot, an ancient card deck used by fortune tellers. In the early medieval period, it is thought the card game bridge evolved using the fifty-two playing cards with the original symbols of the suits. It was believed that nomadic gypsy tribes distributed the playing cards, which promoted the game of bridge. The symbols on the cards indicate the strength and character of each suit, which interestingly correlates with the strength and character of the temperaments.

The exact history and evolution of bridge is controversial, but it is interesting to speculate with regard to the temperaments. Most people understand the hierarchy of suits in our everyday card games, so the correlation of the suits with the temperaments makes the characteristics of the temperaments easier to understand and remember.

The choleric is symbolized by spades. The symbol of spades is the spear head, which is an aggressive weapon for offensive purposes and the show of power. It was used mainly by warriors and war chiefs. The sanguine temperament is symbolized by hearts, which reflect love, warmth, optimism, and openness. The melancholic temperament is symbolized by diamonds. Although this temperament is more passive and negative, it is rich in all the mental, spiritual, and creative forces. The phlegmatic temperament is symbolized by clubs; the club is an unsophisticated, rather dull instrument used for support and defensive purposes. This temperament is primarily the most passive and conservative character, the most calm and the least challenging.

Like in any card game, we must do our best with the cards we are dealt in life. A weak hand comprises mostly minor suits (diamonds and clubs) with few points (positive or strong features). The weak hand is attracted to a partner with a strong hand, which comprises mainly the major suits (spades and hearts). In life, this also holds true, in that people are generally attracted to the opposite type of temperament to maintain balance. Even though the thirteen-card hand dealt in the game of bridge is one of only a finite number of possibilities, the chance of receiving the identical hand again is almost nonexistent. In life, the possible combinations of genes we inherit are nearly infinite, so no one has ever been created exactly like you—in the past, present, or future. You are specially made for a purpose, and must play the hand dealt to you with the best of your ability.

The Correlation of Card Suit to Body Type

Chart 7

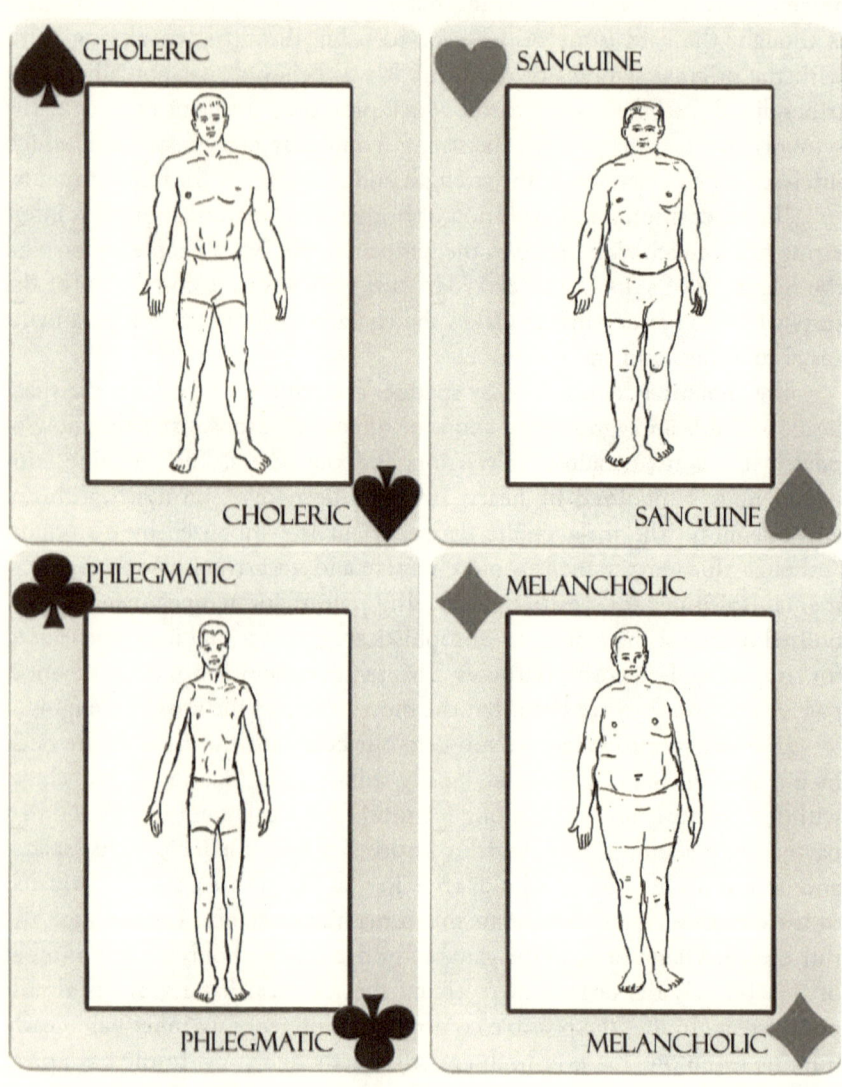

The following information on the dietary and physiological traits of the temperaments has been taken from many sources in addition to my clinical studies, but especially from Rolfe's book.

Distinctive Dietary, Physiologic, and Other Traits

The following descriptions are important considerations in balancing yourself with the proper diet. If you discover your own dominant and secondary temperament, you can alter your diet accordingly to promote a better balance for health and well-being. It must be understood that the food-processing industry is only interested in promoting their products by stimulating your natural cravings, and has little or no concern about nourishment. Processed foods are detrimental to your health and affect your character. It is imperative that you know your individual temperament blend and select the proper foods for optimal health. Ironically, in the ancient world, only the wealthy who indulged in gourmet delicacies (usually refined sugar, starches, creams, and spices) suffered degenerative diseases more than the common folk. The reverse is true today, because processed foods are usually more affordable and available to the general population, who now suffer an alarming rate of degenerative diseases, notably obesity, diabetes, cardiovascular disease, and cancer. A simple diet of unprocessed natural foods, free of chemicals, can be the first and most important step in reestablishing your priorities for optimal health.

In our modern society, we are living longer, but suffering from increased incidence of memory loss, Alzheimer's disease, and obesity. A humorous comment that has a ring of truth states, "Brain cells may die, but fat cells live forever."

1. The Choleric ♠

The choleric temperament, as described by the ancients, is associated with the color red, the sun, heat, and dryness, all of which correlate with the hot or summer season. The choleric, therefore, has a natural affinity for foods that create heat and dryness in the body. Red meat and salt have this effect by creating body heat and building concentrated tissue in the form of muscle. Salt dehydrates the bodily tissues, causing increased thirst and fluid intake. The choleric then eliminates excessive salt, water, and heat by profuse sweating.

The choleric is known to have hyperactive adrenal glands that readily produce hormones in order to respond to stress inside or outside the body. The adrenal hormones increase heart rate, respiration rate, blood pressure, and muscular contraction. At the same time, the adrenal hormones suppress mental function, digestion, pain sensations, and other bodily functions in order to fully respond to any stressful circumstance, emergency, or crisis that may arise. The choleric excels in these situations and in leadership. They love challenges and risks, and have a tendency toward gambling in life. The choleric-dominant temperament is extremely resilient under stress, especially when young, and they are able to go nonstop all day with little sleep. Red meat and salt are the most powerful foods for stimulating the adrenal glands. Distilled alcohol has a similar effect on the adrenal glands. Choleric people rise early in the morning, when they function best, and continue through midday, when the sun is most intense. They exhibit a strong, continuous need for regular, vigorous exercise, which they pursue with zeal. They almost always participate in some kind of athletic activity, and frequently spend much time and energy perfecting body strength, honing athletic skills, and increasing muscle mass.

Due to their circadian rhythm, the adrenals slow down in the afternoon. (See the section on circadian rhythm at the end of this chapter.) In the late afternoon, the choleric-dominant will often desire a heavy cocktail, such as a martini or a salty vodka drink or a margarita, and will usually eat a steak or such for dinner to sustain him or her through the evening. Being goal-oriented, they usually avoid party chatter, turn in early, and sleep less than most people. They are prone to be up at daybreak and devour a heavy breakfast, usually with salted eggs and meat. Cholerics rarely gain weight even though they can consume great volumes of food, mainly due to their exercise habits. They meet the demands and stresses of the day well, managing lots of people with little need for friends or socializing.

Eventually, with time, the adrenal function becomes exhausted, and cholerics on a red meat, salty diet can burn out before their time. Their metabolism naturally slows down as they age and does not respond as well to red meat and salt. Digestive symptoms include heartburn or acid reflux and other gastrointestinal problems. Cholerics will then resort to eating the stimulating food preferences of the subordinate temperament. Sugar becomes the universal craving because it stimulates the depressed system into a manic phase for a few hours. Unless the choleric person becomes more aware of these predispositions and corrects the temperament imbalances, the prognosis for future health and longevity is poor.

2. The Sanguine ♥

The Latin root word in sanguine is "sang," meaning blood. The ancient description of the sanguine temperament linked the natural element of air to blood, in which oxygen is carried. It was believed that breathing was associated with the spirit, which was seated in the heart, where the blood resided. The association of the color orange, air, blood, heart, and spirit characterize the sanguine personality as one that tends toward a free flow of breathing air, who has a serene and optimistic view of life, who has a high level of sexual confidence and libido, and who has a positive attitude toward people and relationships in general. Sanguines tend to be warm, touchy, sensitive, optimistic, joyful, and talkative, possessing an ease of conversation even with strangers. Because of these traits, they are also natural leaders. They are dominated by the sex glands, which, like the adrenals, tend to stimulate the sympathetic nervous system to prepare the body for action and sexual release. The sanguine person is often perceived as hot-blooded, passionate, and ready for action.

The sanguine prefers aphrodisiac foods, such as shellfish, spices, creams, and dark chocolate. When the sanguine feels any kind of stress or lag in energy, it is the sex glands that charge up their metabolism. They learn early in life that aphrodisiac foods boost their energy level.

Sanguines function better in the late afternoon and evening. In humans, sexual activity tends to occur in the evening, and that is when sanguines are more lively and at their best. They tend to stay up late at night, sleep late in the morning, and have a fairly reliable output of energy during the day, but especially enjoy evenings when they are at their best energy level. Even though sanguines are night owls, they do prefer to get a regular eight hours of sleep. They are frequently noted for being tardy for appointments during the day.

Sanguines enjoy a high-fat breakfast, especially eggs; spicy meats, such as sausage or bacon; and creamy fats, such as yogurt, butter, and cheeses. If this type of breakfast stimulates the sex glands too early in the day, it will lead to an excessive appetite and exaggerate their temperament traits all day. This high-fat breakfast in moderation can benefit the sanguine. This meal should consist of unprocessed natural foods that are free of chemicals, and should be eaten later in the morning. Substitute fats such as hydrogenated vegetable oils and substitutes for real cream can be detrimental to the body and the circulatory system. During the day, food intake should be balanced by adding fruits and vegetables and a small amount of refined whole-grain foods. The sanguine metabolism is highly efficient in processing fat, and sanguines do well with fewer calories from refined carbohydrates. They can easily switch to large amounts of sugar and refined carbohydrates to stimulate the thyroid reflection of the secondary melancholic tendencies. In this case, they can put on weight easily and find it difficult to lose weight.

3. The Melancholic ◆

From ancient times, the melancholic temperament was associated with the earth and characterized by creativeness, emotional sensitivity, a volatile mercurial nature, and a preference for bright colors, particularly yellow. The melancholic naturally prefers sugars and starches that are produced by plants from the earth with the help of the sun. Starches are converted to sugar, and all sugar is converted to glucose in the body by the liver. This temperament typically craves sugar and starches every two to three hours during the day, which is the time necessary to obtain a high glucose level and its manic effect, and then for the effect to subside. This cyclic nature of sugar metabolism accounts for the mercurial nature of the melancholic temperament. After ingestion, the high concentration of blood sugar has a drying effect on cells similar to the effect of salt. Water is pulled from the cells to help dilute the blood sugar. This dehydration or drying effect can be damaging to the vascular cells, causing them to be less capable of protecting the body from toxic materials flowing in the blood. This damage to the arterial cells can lead to hardening of the arteries and dangerous plaque formation. All types of temperaments can create these problems if they remain out of balance in their diet by prolonged overindulgence in sugar and refined carbohydrates. However, the melancholic is especially predisposed to these problems.

The compensating mechanism to counter the deleterious effects of dehydration from a sudden influx of sugar is provided by the action of the thyroid gland and the pancreas. When sugar is ingested in concentrated form, blood sugar rises dramatically. This rise stimulates the pancreas to release insulin, which quickly acts on the tissue cells to pull sugar from the blood. The tissue cells will then get dehydrated by the sudden influx of sugar, which could cause damage in the arterial cells if it were not for the thyroid gland. The thyroid gland produces hormones that quickly enhance cellular metabolism. This, in turn, burns up the sugar rapidly to form oxygen and water, thereby preventing cellular destruction from dehydration. The sudden surge in energy the melancholic person experiences after sugar ingestion results from the rapid increase in the thyroid-dependent metabolism. This energy boost, known as a sugar high, generally dissipates within two hours. For this energy level to be maintained would require ingestion of more sugar or a turn to stimulants such as caffeine and nicotine, which act like the thyroid in increasing cellular metabolism.

Melancholics like coffee, cakes, and chocolates for the caffeine's stimulating effect. They favor a high-carbohydrate, low–lean-fat diet, which stimulates their thyroid function and mood. The ongoing cycle of excessive carbohydrate ingestion and subsequent elevated insulin production eventually results in hyperinsulinism, obesity, diabetes, and a host of other conditions, including diseases of the circulatory system and cancer. In the initial stages of hyperinsulinism, it is common to have symptoms of hypoglycemia, prediabetic conditions, and/or developing obesity. These melancholic patients frequently experience mood swings, depression, allergies, and fatigue. They are usually subject to psychiatric treatment when, in fact, dietary and lifestyle changes are necessary to balance their temperament.

4. The Phlegmatic ♣

Hippocrates initially named the four temperaments in accordance with bodily substances, which he thought were primarily responsible for their characteristics. He thought that the choleric had an excess of yellow bile, the sanguine was rich in warm blood, the melancholic was earthy and represented black bile, and the phlegmatic had thick blood and excess mucus, which he called phlegm. The ancients associated the phlegmatic temperament with the element water, and characterized phlegmatics as passive, easygoing, and well-balanced, with a preference for sedate colors, especially blue and gray. Like water, phlegmatics tend to be slow, low-keyed in seeking their own level, and, once positioned, resistant to change. They are naturally cool to matters of life in general. They prefer cool beverages, fruit juices, milk, and mild soups that are not hot. They crave cheese or milk products sweetened with fruit or sugar but notably dislike eggs. They favor occasional snacks over meals on a regular basis. Their basic physiologic predisposition is to conserve energy; this is accomplished primarily by the action of the pituitary gland. This gland directs energy toward body growth rather than metabolic or mental activity. In the phlegmatic, the growth pattern of long bones in the extremities continues well into the late teen years. This accounts for the longer limbs in relation to the trunk length as compared with the other temperaments.

The growing infant, who naturally has elevated growth hormones, may be larger because of an overindulgence in cow's milk, which is also high in pituitary growth hormone. This can account for the comparatively larger children seen in affluent societies as compared with those in underdeveloped countries. This may also be an important factor in the tendency for the phlegmatic child to be tall. In general, the phlegmatic-melancholic blend (PM) are larger people who have a difficult time losing weight, supposedly because of the slow phlegmatic metabolism and the melancholic preference for sugar and starches.

Phlegm, from which the phlegmatic got its name, causes nasal and post-nasal dripping and frequent colds. Because milk somewhat resembles mucus, it can be mucus-forming in some people. This tendency can be lessened by using fermented milk or adding lactose enzymes to the milk. It has been noted that children who overindulge in milk generally do not like vegetables (roughage) because of the uncomfortable bowel cramping they produce. By decreasing the mucus-producing milk intake, these children can become more inclined to eat their vegetables.

Phlegmatics are known to have a sluggish metabolism, and are generally benefited by a high-protein diet, especially one including fish, meats, and eggs with minimal milk. This type of diet will energize and increase their metabolism.

People with the phlegmatic temperament tend to be youthful, late to mature, and somewhat childish well into adulthood. They tend to have a weak sexual libido throughout life. Phlegmatics do not commonly drink to excess, and prefer sweet, milder drinks, such as light beer or wine. However, when they do drink, they are easily inebriated because of their metabolism.

Circadian Rhythm (Body Clock) of the Temperaments

The circadian rhythm or body clock refers to the physiologic rhythm of human bodily functions associated with the twenty-four-hour cycle of the earth's rotation. Scientific information on this subject is well-documented in Dr. Matthew Edlund's book *The Body Clock Advantage.* There are interesting features related to temperaments.

A proper understanding of one's body clock can reveal the best timing for eating, exercise, work, sleep, and even romance and sex to achieve a healthier balance in life. All forms of living things follow the circadian cycle of day and night; however, humans have the choice of living by their inner body clocks.

In preindustrial times, our primarily agricultural society adapted to the biological timing of being awake, alert, and efficient early in the morning after eating the heaviest meal at breakfast with the family. People worked physically until noon and then had a moderate lunch followed by a brief nap or resting period. Work was resumed at a lesser pace until early evening. A light supper was followed by some socialization and then retiring in the later evening, generally between 9:00 PM and 10:30 PM was the norm. The old adage was typical: eat like a king at breakfast, like a prince at lunch, and like a pauper at suppertime.

In our modern industrial society, almost the opposite cultural habits have developed over the past few centuries. Breakfast is often absent or inadequate in nutrition. It may consist of a bagel, a donut, or a roll with coffee and occasionally processed fruit juice. This breakfast of empty calories is usually hurried, not relaxed, and usually eaten without family socialization. Lunch is generally eaten away from home or at work, frequently consisting of fast food or non-nutritional foods, and without subsequent rest. The heaviest meal is at supper in the later evening, usually consisting of foods containing salt, sugar, and fats along with alcoholic drinks. It is the more social time with friends, and is often followed by late-night snacking and possibly more alcoholic drinks.

Insulin sensitivity and increased metabolism associated with cortisol activity is highest in the morning. This occurs when our bodies need the most energy and nutrition to meet the demands of the day. Insulin sensitivity is least efficient in the evening, and, in fact, there is a tendency to insulin resistance at that time. In the evening, there is a diminished metabolic and energy output consistent with decreased cortisol production from the sluggish adrenal cortex. The large meal in late evening, along with late-night snacking, produces unneeded calories that are stored in the fat cells. These cultural habits are most likely the primary cause of the increasing incidence of obesity, diabetes, and cardiovascular disease in our modern industrial society.

It is estimated that the average person in the United States today is sleeping one to one and a half hours less than the body requires for healthy living. Sleep deprivation also increases insulin resistance, which contributes to the increased incidence of diabetes. Metabolisms generally fit into three types:

- Larks, known as morning people
- Owls, known as late-night people
- Switchers, who can adapt to lark or owl habits

The larks represent up to 25 percent of the population, and are characterized by being early morning risers and early night sleepers. They are more alert, productive, and efficient in the morning and early afternoon. They become less alert, energetic, and efficient in the late afternoon and early evening. People who favor the lark's traits are generally choleric-dominants.

The owls represent up to 25 percent of the population, and are characterized by being late-morning risers and late-night sleepers. They do not become alert or efficient until about 10:00 AM, and then they become progressively more alert, energetic, and efficient toward the late evening, night, and even into the early morning hours of the next day. People who favor the owl-like traits are generally sanguine-dominants.

The switchers represent the majority of the population. They will adapt to either the lark or the owl traits depending on the prevalent traits of their employers, partners, or mates. Switchers are generally of the more passive temperaments, the melancholic or the phlegmatic.

Circadian medicine is practiced by physicians who have a specialized knowledge of the inner timing of body physiology. They teach their patients to understand and live by their own inner body clock. In doing so, they produce healthier habits in all areas of life, including proper timing for eating, exercise, work efficiency, sexual activity, sleeping, and achieving weight loss and a maintenance program. Weight loss and maintaining weight loss require proper nutrition and eating habits in accordance with one's circadian metabolism, following the rule of a heavy breakfast, a moderate lunch, and a light supper with no night snacking. Exercise and employing other balancing factors are important in maintaining weight loss.

The graphs in Chart 9 illustrate the relative time differences of the metabolisms of the lark (C) and the owl (S) temperaments.

Chart 8

Figure 1-1: Daily Body Temperature Changes for a Lark

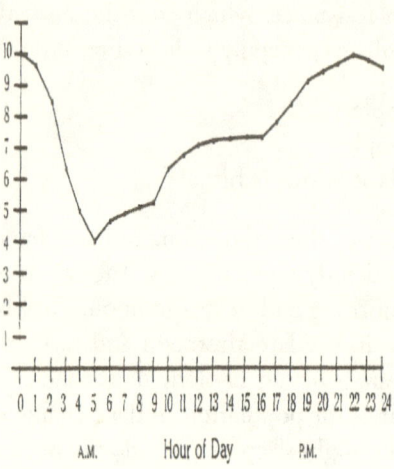

A.M.   Hour of Day   P.M.

Figure 1-3: Daily Body Temperature Changes

LARKS ————

OWLS ————

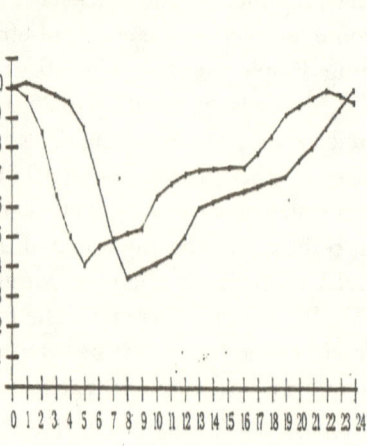

A.M.   Hour of Day   P.M.

Figure 1-2: Daily Body Temperature Changes for an Owl

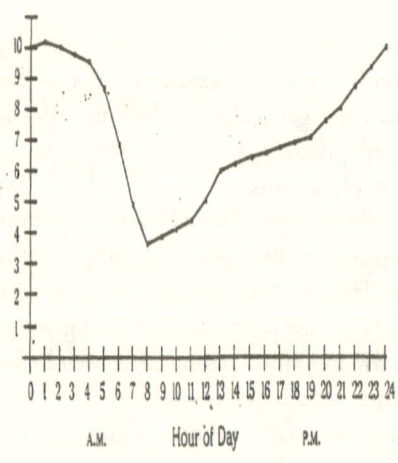

A.M.   Hour of Day   P.M.

Circadian Facts

Major accidents occur most often between midnight and 6:00 AM, when body metabolism is at its lowest. This is true for accidents involving people and industrial accidents. Interestingly, the most well-known industrial accidents and times of their occurrence were Exxon Valdez—12:05 AM, Bhopal chemical plant disaster—2:00 AM, Chernobyl—3:00 AM, and Nine Mile Island nuclear accident—4:00 AM.

Alcohol consumption is more powerful in its effect on the body after midnight. One drink after midnight may be equivalent to two drinks earlier in the day. Alcohol decreases alertness, concentration, and judgment of time, space, and distance, and causes confusion in orientation.

Sleep deprivation combined with alcohol consumption and speeding, especially after midnight, are major factors in fatal automobile accidents. This is especially true for accidents involving teenagers or young people who are risk-oriented choleric-dominants.

The best period for harmonious relationships between larks and owls is the overlap time between early afternoon and early evening.

Partners or mates who are extreme opposites in their body clock timing (i.e., larks versus owls) can be successfully treated to shift their inner body clock timing with the proper use of light therapy, exercise, and the drug melatonin.

Adequate sleep of approximately eight hours per twenty-four-hour period is required by most people to maintain a healthy life style. Sleep deprivation of one and a half to two hours per night is present in most of the U.S. population, especially in people under forty years of age. Sleep deprivation strongly contributes to problems of stress, reduced alertness, inefficiency at work, and poor weight control.

Sleep occurs in cycles of approximately ninety minutes, and each cycle consists of several stages. The last stage is called REM, for rapid eye movement, and is the most important stage to receive adequate rest and maintain healthy physiological functions of the body.

Cycles of Nature and Weather

There are many cycles that occur in nature that affect humanity. It is beyond the scope of this book to delve into them. However, it is important to study and understand these cycles because they play a vital role in human adaptation, survival, and evolution. These cycles occur naturally within our bodies and include biorhythms, menstruation, fertility, pregnancy, and bodily adaption to changes in seasons, environment, and climate. The cycles of nature that are manifested outside our bodies can vitally affect humans. These cycles include lunar cycles, cycles of sunspots, cycles of war, economic cycles, and cycles of weather change involving storms and hurricanes that can threaten our existence. These subjects are covered in great detail in a most interesting book called *Climate and the Affairs of Men,* by Winkless and Browning.

In my office I kept a weather instrument that recorded temperature, humidity, and barometric pressure. I learned over the years that weather changes affected the behavior of my patients and determined the outcome of my day. I noted that people were pleasant and easy to care for when the day was sunny and clear, the temperature was between 70 and 85 degrees, and the barometric pressure was 30 or more. I also noted that people were more negative, irritable, and depressed when the day was wet, dreary, gloomy, and overcast; when the temperature was above 85 degrees or below 70 degrees; when the humidity was over 80 percent; and when the barometric pressure was below 30.

I learned the hard way to avoid any heavy discussions on those dreary days, such as contemplation of surgery or uncomfortable procedures, questionable diagnoses and prognoses, procedural costs, and especially their medical bills or delinquent accounts.

CHAPTER VII

Historical Highlights of the Temperaments

The purpose of this chapter is not to elaborate on the history of the temperaments, but to affirm with a historical summary that people have probed this fascinating subject since the beginning of recorded history. Hippocrates (460–370 BC), known as the father of medicine, is credited with initially documenting and naming the four temperaments. He possessed a keen ability to accurately observe and record human traits, including physical, emotional, mental, and spiritual qualities of the whole person. He classified and named the temperaments into four groups that he observed clinically—choleric, sanguine, melancholic, and phlegmatic.

Hippocrates associated these names and characteristics with the four elements of the universe: choleric with fire, sanguine with air, melancholic with earth, and phlegmatic with water. He further associated the temperaments with various bodily humors, which he described as follows: choleric with yellow bile, sanguine with blood, melancholic with black bile, and phlegmatic with lymph or phlegm. Although these references may appear ambiguous at first, researchers of the temperaments believe that such descriptive humors refer to energies that influence the functions of the body, emotions, mind, and spirit. The four temperaments were also correlated with the four seasons: choleric with summer, being hot and dry; sanguine with spring, being warm and wet; melancholic with autumn, being cool and dry; and phlegmatic with winter, being cold and wet. (A more detailed treatment of these associations is found in chapter I.) As you learn more about temperaments, you will see the importance of these relationships to physical and mental well-being.

Hippocrates' method of observing and describing disorders or unbalances of the humors is considered to be the beginning of modern medicine. His philosophy of health and disease was based on the imbalance of the four humoral temperaments. He and his followers were proponents of a connection between physique, temperament, and predisposition to certain diseases. They proposed that human studies must integrate all aspects of human observations, both in health and in disease. This view would certainly question the modern wisdom of studying one aspect, such as mental function, in isolation from a perspective of the whole person and the inherent temperamental predisposition.

These ideas of associating physique, temperament, and disease predisposition have been accepted and rejected over the centuries. Many researchers published reports of these associations, but these reports eventually lost credibility because they lacked accepted scientific proof. Tim LaHaye, in his book *Transformed Temperaments,* credited Dr. W. Wandt with establishing the concept of constitutional psychology at Leipzig University in 1879. Dr. Wandt performed exhaustive studies attributing man's personality traits to his body structure. Unfortunately, he tried to be too exacting, and consequently failed.

As mentioned in the introduction to this book, Dr. Ernst Kretschmer and his study of physique and character also failed to gain widespread recognition. Despite the repeated failures, the idea of the association between physique and temperament has also prevailed throughout the ages.

In 1942, Dr. W. H. Sheldon published his book *The Varieties of Temperament,* in which he reduced the number of physical types associated with character to three types: mesoderm, endoderm, and ectoderm. This concept was later altered to include the fourth physical type, known as sanguine, which represents a composite of mesoderm and endoderm.

The essential reason for the failure of the various publications on constitutional psychology is that the complexities of the various mixtures of human temperaments and the numerous environmental influences make it impossible to completely scientifically describe and classify these associations. This, however, does not preclude the fact that, for all practical purposes, there is a definite relationship between physique, temperament, and predispositions to disease. The work of many artists, caricaturists, dramatists, and novelists has subscribed to these associations. Authors and followers of Hippocrates have documented these associations for centuries. These relationships were the primary basis of Western medicine for more than two thousand years, yet, unbelievably, little of this has been known, recognized, or taught in modern medical education for the last two hundred years because there is no actual scientific support concerning these observations. However, anecdotal evidence by astute medical clinicians and observers attest to these observations.

These relationships and associations are well-documented in *The Four Temperaments,* by Randy Rolfe. Certain prominent historical figures over the last two thousand years were outstanding proponents of the temperament theory and their associations.

The history of the temperaments and their humors is vast. Some of the ancient masters who believed in this theory include Aristotle (384–322 BC), Galen (Claudius Galenus) (130–201 AD), Hidegard of Bingen (1097–1179 AD), and Albert Magnus (1193–1280 AD). Geoffrey Chaucer (1345–1400

AD), famous for his work *The Canterbury Tales*, and William Shakespeare (1564–1616 AD) were known to promote their belief in the temperament and humoral theories of Hippocrates. Paracelsus (1493–1541 AD), a Swiss-German philosopher, physician, and teacher, wrote exhaustive works on the four humors and temperaments.

Interest in the temperament theory dwindled with the advent of Sigmund Freud, who popularized the theory of behavior and psychoanalytical psychiatry. Carl Jung, who was a psychoanalyst and student of Freud, consequently introduced a simplified classification of temperaments. This classifications was popularized over the past century—namely, Type A, representing an extrovert personality, and Type B, representing an introvert personality.

In the 1940s, Katherine Briggs adopted her own theory of sixteen types of personalities based on the Jungian system. She and her daughter, Isobel Myers, developed and published a questionnaire about preferences that is now known as the Myers-Briggs Type Indicator (MBTI). This method of analysis is presently used widely as a psychological instrument. In 1978, David Keirsey, an American psychologist, revived the temperament theory in his book *Please Understand Me.* He correlated the four temperaments with the sixteen Myers-Briggs personality types.

Among the several different behavior theories from Jung's two types to the Myers-Briggs sixteen types, the four-temperament theory of Hippocrates still appears to be the best and easiest to understand and use for self-understanding and self-improvement. All other theories are essentially derivations of Hippocrates' original theory.

In recent years, the tide is changing. The theories of Darwinian evolution, Freudian psychology, and behaviorism are declining in popularity. Although the contributions of Freud did confirm the skill to diagnose personality problems, questions were raised regarding their ability to heal the disorders efficiently. A new breed of psychiatrists, psychologists, and scientists is rekindling an interest in the Hippocrates theory, which emphasizes the responsibility of people for their own behavior.

The temperament theory has survived for twenty-four hundred years and has always been prevalent in Europe. In modern times, the study of disease focuses primarily on pathology and environment. The influence of the whole person (mind, body, and spirit) on disease development is often neglected because of reliance on diagnostic technology. Holistic medicine came into being as a response to this lack of integrated perspective in modern medicine.

My practice of dermatology and internal medicine with an interest in general medicine was fertile ground to consider and examine aspects of the whole person, because it reflects all fields of medicine. The subject matter in this book is dealt with in a general manner and does not involve detailed statistical analysis, which was not feasible or possible in a private practice. It does not profess to be scientific or precise; nevertheless, it recognizes and professes, as a relative truth, the relationship between body build, personality, and disease predisposition.

PART TWO

DISEASE PREDISPOSITIONS OF THE FOUR TEMPERAMENTS

CHAPTER VIII

Disease and Disorders Frequently Associated with the Dominant Temperaments

Prologue

Holistic medicine has been in vogue over the past few decades. It implies that the mind, body, and spirit are interconnected in determining our behavior, state of health, and longevity. Clinical researchers have always attempted to associate body build with temperament (constitutional medicine). Despite the repeated failures of scientific and schematic classifications, the idea of a fundamental connection between physique, temperament, and disease predisposition has persisted since the time of Hippocrates. Prior to the mid-twentieth century, many great physicians and clinicians firmly believed that the physical form of the individual bears an important relationship to disease. Draper, in his monograph on the subject, emphasized that the central doctrine of Greek medicine and the concepts of Hippocrates should be reconsidered more seriously in present-day medical education. He reiterated that the inherited physical features of the individual are related to the physiological, psychological, and immunological aspects. These factors, together with the lesser influence of environment, make up the constitution that determines one's reaction to stress or injury. As stated in the introduction, during the course of my forty years of clinical practice, more than five hundred patients were documented, evaluated, and diagnosed physically with a special reference as to my impression of their constitutional temperaments. A careful history of personal and family medical history was included in the clinical evaluation. A formula for the constitutional temperament was devised and recorded during the initial examination. It used the first letter of each temperament to indicate the temperament mix (i.e., C, S, M, P, representing choleric, sanguine, melancholic, and phlegmatic). The first letter in the formula represented the most dominant characteristic, and the last letter represented the least-observed temperament. For all practical purposes, only the first two (primary dominant and secondary subdominant) are clinically discernable, and the last two temperaments are mostly indiscernible or insignificant. My impression of the first two temperaments was correct in approximately 80 percent of the cases, although not necessarily in the same order as indicated in the psychological test.

In my study, men were primarily considered, because many serious organic diseases occur in men, and men have been studied more than women. Diseases found to be more common in men include those of the gastrointestinal tract, the respiratory tract, blood vessels, heart, bones, joints, and urinary tract. Notable exceptions where diseases are more common in women include gallbladder disease, thyroid disease, Raynaud's syndrome, hypertension, and certain functional diseases, such as fibromyalgia, migraines, hysteria, and chronic nervous exhaustion. It is known that there is a higher mortality among males throughout all periods of life, especially during intrauterine and early childhood life. This sex-linked weakness from conception to death exists throughout the animal kingdom.

Information on the predisposition to disease in the various temperaments was derived from my personal clinical experience and from a review of authentic medical journals, periodicals, and textbooks. Unfortunately, in the twentieth century, such information was not often scientifically documented; therefore, temperament theory was scarcely mentioned in the medical literature.

Common sense and practical observation of human nature cannot be disregarded, even though it is not considered scientific. The scientific method of investigation utilizes data to arrive at a probable cause or explanation of a disease process. Admittedly, it is a valuable tool, although it cannot be exact or definitive, because it does not in itself explain the meanings of vital phenomenon. On the other hand, the Hippocratic theory of temperaments, although not exact, is supported by the test of time, is understandable, conveys meaning, and suggests methods of treatment for balancing the whole person.

In my practice, all temperaments were observed, but the largest number consisted of the sanguine and melancholic dominant type. I observed a lesser number of the phlegmatic dominant type, and the smallest number was of the choleric dominant type.

The following lists and descriptions of diseases have a definite association with a person's constitution. Examples of diseases under each temperament are minimal at best when one considers the general absence of information in modern literature regarding a constitutional connection with the vast number of human infirmities. Perhaps with the advent of newer technological advances, this type of report may stimulate future scientifically based research concerning the role of constitution in disease development (constitutional medicine).

Disease Predispositions

1. The Choleric ♠

It was apparent that the smallest numbers of my patients were choleric-dominant, and most of those were teenagers, usually presenting mild to moderate acne. A few of the males, especially, presented marked cystic, scar-forming acne. Most of the choleric-dominant patients were disease free during their youth, and only a few had minor dermatologic disorders. The choleric-dominant temperament is known to have hyperactivity of the anterior pituitary gland and especially the adrenal cortex. The hyperactivity of both glands probably accounts for the energetic personality and high level of physical endurance.

A high percentage of choleric-dominant patients are seen by the sports medical specialist and the orthopedic surgeon for physical conditions related to muscle, bone, tendon, and joint disturbances, especially from injury and broken bones. Because of their love of sports, adventure, and risk-taking activities, cholerics are more prone to fractures involving all areas of the bony structure, notably the extremities, hips, pelvis, spinal column, shoulders, and feet. The incidences of paraplegias and quadriplegias are very high in the athletic choleric-dominant person. This is true of tendonitis occurring in various areas of the body as well. Common diagnoses due to stress and injury include popliteal, or behind the knee, tendonitis; Achilles tendonitis; Achilles tendon fracture; runners' knee; hamstring injury; tennis elbow; and rotary cuff tendonitis. Choleric-dominant men heavily outnumber choleric-dominant women among the injured.

Dupuytren's contracture is a progressive shrinking of the bands of fibrous tissue inside the palms, producing a curling of the fingers that eventually results in a clawlike hand. The right hand is usually affected, and in the few instances where both hands are involved, the right hand is more severely affected. Although this condition can occur in other dominant temperaments, it is believed to be an inherent condition that is more common and more severe in the choleric-dominant male. In about half the cases, it is associated with penile fibromatosis (Peyronie's disease), which contracts and deforms the penis, distorting the shape of an erection. In some instances, there is no known disease, but alcoholism (and, to a lesser degree, diabetes) may be a precipitating factor.

Diseases of the bones are more common among choleric-dominant patients, especially men. This includes bone tumors, both benign and malignant. The most common benign tumors are the noneventful ostemos; however, an uncommon painful benign giant cell tumor involving bone may be a crippling problem. The serious and life-threatening bone malignancies are seen mostly in choleric-dominant men and include osteosarcomas of the extremities, multiple myeloma, and malignant lymphoma.

Metastatic bone tumors do not necessarily involve choleric-dominant patients, and the most likely are metastatic lesions of the breast, lung, prostate, kidney, and thyroid. Any bone may be involved, but usually not beyond the knee or elbow.

Acromegaly is a rare, clinical manifestation of an extreme choleric constitution equally expressed in both sexes. It results from an overproduction of growth hormone, usually caused by a benign pituitary tumor (adenoma). In children, before the growth plates have closed, excessive production of the growth hormone leads to gigantism, which is manifested by a rapid growth of the long bones, usually leading to a very large stature. In adulthood, after the growth plates have closed, usually between the ages of thirty and fifty, the bony deformities resulting from the excessive growth hormone is called acromegaly. In adulthood, bones throughout the body thicken, which is especially obvious in marked exaggeration of facial features, hands, and feet. Abraham Lincoln was thought by some medical practitioners to have had this condition. All elements of the skin, musculature, and connective tissue involving internal organs enlarge, and eventually produce symptoms related to impingement of nerves. The diagnosis is confirmed by the obvious clinical manifestation along with X-rays and blood tests that usually show high levels of growth hormone.

Paget's disease of the bone is also a rare condition that appears to primarily affect the choleric-dominant individual. It occurs mainly in men of northern Europe extraction, generally after the age of forty. It appears to be a genetic condition where the cells that remove and replace the bone are overactive, producing bone pain, enlargement, and deformity, often involving the head. Hearing loss, dizziness, and headaches can result. Other bone structures, such as vertebrae and extremities, can be involved, leading to fractures and a poor prognosis. High blood calcium and alkaline phosphatase are notable features in the diagnosis.

After fifty years of age, if the choleric-dominant person has not balanced their temperament, they may exhibit diseases associated with adrenal insufficiency, producing a lack of cortisone in the body (burned-out adrenal function). This can lead to obscure connective tissue disorders that may be dramatically incapacitating.

Fibromyalgia is an obscure functional condition more commonly diagnosed in women, but usually more serious in men. Choleric-dominant men who have consistently indulged in excessive alcohol consumption over the years may suffer from this condition, which is characterized by stiffness and pain in localized areas such as the jaw, neck, and shoulder muscles. It may progress to become more generalized throughout the body. This is more likely to occur in men who engage in physical, muscular activities in their occupation or in sports. The condition may be worsened by mental stress, poor sleep, repetitive strains and injuries, or chronic exposure to dampness and cold. General systematic treatments, along with alleviating physical and mental stress, are indicated. Nonsteroidal anti-inflammatory drugs are generally of limited benefit. The use of systemic steroids and possibly antidepressants may be necessary to control this disabling disease.

The choleric-dominant individual exhibits the Type A extroversive, hard-driving behavior, and is more prone to heart attacks. They often have high levels of triglycerides and cholesterol in their blood. The somewhat dark, dusky, and yellowish hue of facial skin, along with the occasional development of xanthelasma (yellow plaque) of the lower eyelids, reflects high blood lipids (hyperlipoproteinemia). Abnormal levels of lipids, especially cholesterol, requiring the use of cholesterol-lowering drugs for control, can lead to long-term problems such as atherosclerosis (hardening of the arteries), heart attacks, and strokes. Factors other than the inherent ones that adversely affect lipid levels include normal aging, being overweight, smoking, a high-stress lifestyle, a diet high in fat and low in fiber, and daily indulgence in moderate to excessive alcohol consumption. Not infrequently, the choleric-dominant gains weight with aging, especially around the upper body, chest, and shoulders.

Another common systematic condition that appears to be prevalent among the choleric-dominant is acid reflux disease. It would be interesting to discover whether this is an inherent weakness in the esophageal sphincter and gastric hyperacidity. A prolonged history of acid reflux disease certainly predisposes to esophageal problems, especially esophageal cancer. Aspiration pneumonia occurring after eating late at night could be a rare but serious complication. Effective systematic treatment primarily involves the use of antacids and drugs to reduce gastric acid.

Kretschmer, in his study of two thousand institutionalized mental patients, found the choleric-dominant temperament rarely had a psychosis, but when present, it was usually a psychopathic disorder, or schizophrenia if they had a phlegmatic subdominant temperament.

Throughout my career, I have witnessed several male patients with a diagnosis of either pancreatitis or pancreatic cancer. It is my recollection that they all had in common a choleric constitution. Hopefully, future research will be able to substantiate these observations, and also determine whether excess alcohol intake played a part in the etiology.

The hard-driving choleric-dominant temperament must learn to rebalance, slow down emotionally and physically, and eat a balanced diet containing more vegetables, fiber, and quality fats. They must learn to eat less, curb their drinking of hard liquor, and avoid smoking. Otherwise the prognosis for a long life, free of serious disease, is unlikely.

2. The Sanguine ♥

The sanguine may suffer a variety of physical problems, which they generally tend to minimize. They exhibit diseases that are usually moderate in severity, chronic in nature, slower-developing, and as a rule, not life-threatening.

Sleep apnea is frequently observed in the sanguine-dominant individual. Because of the importance of the element air to sanguines, they may suffer inadequate oxygenation of the tissues. The short thick neck, thick chest, and large abdomen may contribute to the symptoms of sleep apnea. This condition is often diagnosed after reports from the person's sleep partner. Such reports may include loud snoring, periodic cessation of breathing, and awakening from deep sleep with apprehension and/or choking. The disturbance of sleep can result in daytime sleepiness, fatigue, irritability, and morning headaches. They may often fall asleep while watching TV, while attending meetings, and even while driving. This condition can cause symptoms of memory impairment, decreased libido, and difficulty concentrating. Aggravating factors include obesity, smoking, excessive use of alcohol and mind-altering drugs, chronic lung disease, and any obstructive condition of the respiratory tract. If the correction of these factors does not eliminate or relieve sleep apnea, these people may benefit from the use of continuous positive airway pressure (C-PAP). This is prescribed after a sleep laboratory examination and only by a qualified sleep specialist.

Common maladies in the sanguine-dominant involve frequent muscle and soft tissue discomfort and pain. Arthritic changes in the neck associated with pain and generalized osteoarthritic changes in the major joints are common causes of stiffness and discomfort. (As in sleep apnea, the lack of oxygen intake may also contribute to these maladies.) Degenerative osteoarthritis of the hip is a common problem in the sanguine-dominant. When physical therapy, exercise, and the use of simple analgesics and anti-inflammatory drugs fail to relieve the pain, some joints may be successfully replaced by an artificial joint. Improvement in motion, function, and a decrease in pain is usually dramatic in patients who undergo hip replacement.

Soreness and numbness of the hands, especially from carpal tunnel syndrome, is frequently encountered in the sanguine-dominant, particularly in women. This syndrome is a painful compression of the median nerve as it passes through the wrist. Symptoms include numbness, tingling, and pain in the first three fingers on the thumb side of the hand. People at risk usually work in jobs requiring repeated forceful movements of the hands with the wrist extended. This condition is often encountered with concomitant pregnancy, diabetes, underactive thyroid, gout, or arthritis. Trigger finger is often present in people with carpal tunnel syndrome. In this condition, a finger becomes locked in a bent position; this occurs when a tendon of that finger becomes swollen and tender. A local injection of corticosteriod with a local anesthetic or surgery is needed to correct the condition. Painful feet, especially from bone spurs with fasciitis or arthritic bone changes, are common among sanguine-dominant patients. Not infrequently, arthritis of the toes and hammertoe are also observed.

It is not uncommon for the sanguine male to develop an inguinal hernia. This occurs when a loop of intestines on either side of the groin pushes through a weakness in the opening of the abdominal wall that leads to the inguinal canal. The inguinal canal contains the vas deferens, blood vessels, nerves, and other structures connected to the testicles. A bulge gradually enlarges on the affected side, and surgical correction is necessary to prevent progressive enlargement, pain, and discomfort. The protruding obese abdomen of the sanguine contributes to the development of inguinal hernia. Reducing abdominal obesity or wearing a garment to reduce pressure on the involved inguinal canal is beneficial in relieving the symptoms.

Hiatus hernia is a common condition among people over sixty years of age. It is a protrusion of a portion of stomach that occurs through a weakness in the diaphragm that separates the upper esophagus from the lower stomach. The condition is usually asymptomatic, but may produce symptoms of indigestion, typically when a person lies down after eating a full meal. Simple measures of treatment most often relieve the symptoms, such as elevation of the head, antacids, and drugs to reduce gastric acidity. Rarely is surgical repair necessary. It is believed to be more prevalent in sanguine persons, possibly because of inherent tendencies to develop hernias, weakening of the bodily sphincters, and a protuberant obese abdomen.

Prostate problems develop in most men over fifty, and there is no known documentation of a prevalence of prostate problems in any particular temperament dominance. However, there is a general impression among clinicians that the obese sanguine frequently exhibits prostate problems, particularly benign hypertrophy of the prostate with associated urinary symptoms.

Mild allergies are usually seen in the sanguine child, but not predominantly in that temperament. The dermatologic manifestations of the sanguine temperament are rather vast and comprise a large part of a dermatology practice. The majority of my acne patients were sanguine-dominant, with various degrees of severity of acne during the teenage period. Overactivity of the oil glands as a result of hormonal stimulation is primarily responsible for the development of acne and the associated prevalence of dandruff, oiliness, and seborrhea dermatitis of the scalp, face, and upper trunk. In adulthood, over-activity of the oil glands associated with flushing of the midface is common-ly seen in sanguine people of Celtic or northern Europe descent. Persistent redness, visible superficial blood vessels, small pimples, and thickened skin around the nose are characteristic features known as rosacea. This condition is more common during and after middle age, especially in women. When men are affected, a more severe type can be manifested, frequently with the development of a red, bulbous nose called rhinophyma. This condition is particularly common in alcoholics. Factors that aggravate rosacea include spicy foods, alcohol, coffee, caffeinated drinks, stress, and sunlight, to which sanguines are usually sensitive. Understanding and balancing the sanguine temperament is important in the management of this condition. Rosacea is frequently associated with diabetes and psoriasis.

Often, Type II diabetes and obesity are observed among the sanguine-dominant temperament. It usually begins in people who are older than thirty and becomes progressively more common with age. In Type II diabetes, the body develops resistance to the effect of insulin, so that there is not enough insulin to meet the body's need. It tends to run in families, and is twice as prevalent in blacks and Hispanics in the United States. Obesity is the chief risk factor for developing Type II diabetes. The symptoms of diabetes may be subtle, and the disease may not be diagnosed for decades. Gradually, the occurrence of symptoms increases, including extreme fatigue, blurred vision, drowsiness, decreased endurance and libido, excessive urination (polyuria) associated with abnormal thirst (polydipsia), and a multitude of other sub-jective symptoms. Treatment of diabetes involves diet, weight loss, exercise, education, and, for most diabetic patients, drugs to control blood sugar and sometimes blood cholesterol and lipids. Uncontrolled diabetes leads to com-plications, primarily from narrowing of blood vessels that results in athero-sclerosis, which progressively decreases blood supply to all tissues, especially to the skin and nerves. Over a period of time, poor circulation can harm the heart, brain, legs, eyes, kidneys, nerves, and skin. Heart attacks and strokes are common. Poor circulation of the skin can lead to ulcers, infections, and various skin manifestations of diabetes. All wounds heal slowly. Bacterial, fungal, and yeast infections frequently occur in the moist areas of the body.

Benign skin growths are common in the sanguine temperament, especially when associated with obesity and diabetes. These are small, flesh-colored or brown skin tags predominantly on the neck, but also seen on the eyelids, trunk, armpits, and groin. They occur frequently with seborrhea keratoses, which are light brown to black, oval, small warty legions that are loosely attached to the skin. A rare condition primarily seen in obese sanguine women, especially with a diabetic tendency, is called pseudoacanthosis nigricans. This condition presents a grayish velvety thickening of the skin on the sides of the neck, axillae, and groin. It is reversible when the patient attains normal weight.

Psoriasis is common among the sanguine-dominant temperament. It occurs in both sexes, primarily in whites of European descent, and generally in people aged ten to forty. It is a chronic, reoccurring disease characterized by one or more slightly raised red patches with silvery scales mainly seen on the scalp, elbows, knees, back, or buttocks. Psoriasis may flair up for no apparent reason, but usually as a result of a variety of circumstances, such as minor injuries, sunburn, infections, wintertime, and stress. Sometimes, excessive alcohol consumption and drugs such as antimalarials, lithium, and beta blockers can cause psoriasis to flare.

Gout is a rather common disorder often seen in the obese sanguine male. Gout most often affects the joints in the feet, particularly the base of the big toe, although other joints are also commonly affected, such as the ankle, knee, wrist, and elbow. It presents as a painful, swollen joint inflammation that results from deposits of sodium urate crystals because of high levels of blood uric acid. A high-purine diet and/or high alcohol consumption are usually the causative factors, and the condition generally responds dramatically to treatment.

A heavy chest and large liver are associated with the sanguine patient. They are predisposed to diseases of the liver leading to cirrhosis. An obese sanguine with diabetes often exhibits a fatty liver, which is susceptible to toxins, especially alcohol consumption. The sanguine constitution is prevalent among people of southern European and Mediterranean extraction. Their preference for moderate wine consumption and the avoidance of hard liquor is well-known, and possibly represent a natural defense against any liver toxicity. The sanguine's basic humor is blood, as described by Hippocrates. Interestingly, the sanguine has a predisposition to several blood diseases, such as polycythemia vera, hemochromatosis, and lymphomas.

A form of late neurosyphilis is called paresis and is more likely to occur in the sanguine (pyknic) type. This is a rare progressive disease affecting the brain cells, leading to gradual behavior changes, such as grandiose feelings, deterioration in personal hygiene, mood swings, and progressive confusion.

Draper noted from his studies of temperament and gallbladder disease that 80 percent of the gallbladder cases were in women of the sanguine-melancholic (SM) temperament. He further noted that infantile paralysis (poliomyelitis) was more common in the sanguine-dominant patient.

Kretschmer, in his studies of institutionalized psychotic patients, found that the cyclic or manic-depressive type of psychosis occurred predominantly in the sanguine-melancholic temperament. He referred to them as the "pyknic" type.

3. The Melancholic ♦

In a dermatologic practice, it is common to observe certain skin diseases peculiar to the melancholic-dominant person. They often exhibit wide mood swings in their mercurial personality, which is also reflected in a labile immune system. This is manifested by frequent episodes of acute disease disorders. Viral infections such as recurrent herpes simplex, viral upper respiratory infections (colds), influenza (flu), and acute tonsillitis, are common. It is not unusual to observe bacterial infections of the skin and soft tissues, such as impetigo, furunculosis (boils), and cellulitis, as well as fungal and yeast infections in the intertriginous areas of the hands, feet, and groin.

The melancholic-dominant person is commonly susceptible to allergies. The immune system can overreact to certain antigens (called allergens) that are harmless in most people. The result is an allergic reaction to one or many substances. These allergens may cause an allergic reaction when they contact the skin or the eyes, or are inhaled, eaten, or injected. It may be a seasonal allergy (such as hay fever) caused by exposure to such substances as grass or ragweed. Allergic reactions may be triggered by chemicals and toxins either externally or internally. Various manifestations of allergic reactions in the body are seen as allergic contact dermatitis, localized neurodermatitis, dermagraphism, hives, and chronic urticaria. In some rare cases, anaphylaxis may occur, which is a sudden, widespread, potentially severe and life-threatening allergic reaction more commonly caused by a drug such as penicillin, insect stings, certain foods, or allergy injections (allergen immunotherapy).

Vasomotor instability is commonly observed in the melancholic-dominant person, especially when in association with the choleric or phlegmatic subdominant. This is manifested as erythema (purplish red color) of the extremities, particularly of the palms and soles of the feet, which also feel cold and, at times, sweaty. These symptoms worsen with exposure to cold and with increased emotional stress. It is seen more often in women and is a feature of atopic dermatitis in both sexes.

Atopic dermatitis is frequently observed as a symptom of the atopic constitution, which includes eczema, dry skin, hay fever, asthma, allergic rhinitis, and a family history of similar conditions. Many factors can cause atopic dermatitis to flare up, such as emotional stress, changes in environmental temperature or humidity, contact with wool or other irritating fabrics, viral or bacterial infections, and occasionally food allergies. The personality characteristics and emotional makeup of the atopic person predominates among the melancholic-dominant individual. The combination of the melancholic- and choleric-dominant temperaments is commonly observed among the atopic patients. This blend would account for the negative imbalanced features of both temperaments, which include being oversensitive, easily depressed, intolerant, tense, self-assertive, hypochrondriacal, and hyperactive until completely exhausted.

Allergies and episodes of acute infections tend to lessen and even disappear in adulthood. However, they are often replaced by other conditions, such as frequent headaches and gastrointestinal problems. These include a tendency to gastric or duodenal ulcers, to duodenitis (Crohn's disease), colitis, and irritable bowel syndrome. Yeast infections in the moist areas and vaginal areas in women, especially in obese diabetic persons, are frequent conditions in adulthood.

Thyroid problems are common in the melancholic person, especially in older women. A condition often found among older women is hypothyroidism, which is underactivity of the thyroid gland that leads to inadequate production of the thryroid hormone and a slowing of vital body functions. The causes of hypothyroidism include various forms of thyroiditis, treatment of hyperthyroidism with radioactive iodine or surgical removal of the thyroid, a deficiency of iodine in the diet, and, in some cases, an inherited disorder. Thyroid replacement therapy plus adequate intake of iodine in the diet is necessary in these instances.

A predisposition to hypoglycemia and diabetes are common threats to the melancholic-dominant person. In hypoglycemia the blood sugar level becomes too low, and in diabetes the blood sugar level becomes too high. Many people with diabetes periodically experience hypoglycemia also. In fact, hypoglycemia is usually a sign of the onset of diabetes, and is rare without oncoming diabetes.

The effects of aging on joints and bones are present in all people, but are especially frequent conditions in the adult melancholic person, particularly women after menopause. The main changes producing symptoms in the joints and bones include accelerated loss of bone density (osteoporosis) and brittleness of the cartilage and connective tissues of the ligaments and tendons of the joints. These changes lead to stiffer joints and increased susceptibility to injury, and may often progress to osteoarthritis. The changes in the joints and bones are also associated with a gradual loss of voluntary muscle mass (sarcopenia) and muscle strength. Regular exercise and the adequate consumption of calcium and vitamin D are useful in preventing and treating these conditions. Hormone replacement therapy may also be indicated.

The predispositions described here may be the result of an inherent melancholic constitution, and also of the indulgent lifestyle, which includes the desire for sugar and refined carbohydrates, including pastries, pasta, beer, and wine. The melancholic-dominant frequently gives a history of overuse of medications, such as stimulants and sedatives. The cold, dry season of fall usually produces the worst symptoms, consistent with their humoral characteristics. They have a tendency toward mental depression and withdrawal. Kretschmer observed in his studies that when psychosis developed in the melancholic-dominant, it was predominantly of the manic-depressive type. During the autumn season, they frequently suffer symptoms of sinus problems, bronchial infections, migraine headaches, and major allergic symptoms due to mold from trees. The earthy nature of melancholics makes them more susceptible to seasonal affective disorder (cabin fever or winter blues) and to weather changes during this period. Their moods are highly affected by low barometric pressure and dark, overcast, and high-humidity days.

4. The Phlegmatic ♣

Phlegmatic-dominant people are described as being ascetic in constitution, which means weak, with slender limbs and body. Kretschmer noted in his study that they may perform only satisfactorily in minor athletics, but are often great walkers and swimmers. They have notably low blood pressure and low metabolism. They generally have a relatively disease-free childhood. This is believed to be attributable to their natural dominant activity of the pituitary gland.

During early childhood, phlegmatics often develop infections, especially of the respiratory tract. Pharyngitis (sore throat) is a common occurrence, and is caused by the same viruses that cause the common cold. At times, a more serious cause of pharyngitis is due to the streptococcus bacteria (strep throat). The tonsils and adenoids (lymphoid tissue at the back of the throat) can be involved in either case to produce fever, swelling, and infection of the throat and lymph glands in the neck. If the swelling of the throat tissue (tonsils and adenoids) is severe enough, it may lead to obstructive symptoms of the upper respiratory tract, producing middle ear and sinus problems. In chronic cases, phlegmatics may develop changes in the palate with a "pinched nose" quality to the voice, disturbance of the teeth, and obstructive sleep apnea. In most cases, the upper respiratory infection is mild and limited, requiring only systemic care. With strep infections, scarlet fever, and other infectious diseases, antibiotics may be indicated, along with the removal of the tonsils and adenoids in the chronic stages.

The phlegmatic-dominant temperament, especially when associated with a secondary melancholic temperament, is prone to develop conditions more related to the melancholic. Their primary personality traits favor the phlegmatic characteristics, but their physical traits, though not as pronounced, express melancholic characteristics. Asthma, hay fever, eczema, and related skin disorders are common. Various forms of allergies may appear, such as allergic contact dermatitis, allergic insect bites, dermagraphia, hives, and urticaria (giant hives). Occasionally, allergies to dust, animal dander, molds, and certain foods or drugs are evident in this temperament. A marked itching and uncommon skin condition called lichenplanus is more prevalent in the phlegmatic-melancholic association. Relative obesity, hypothyroidism, hypoglycemia, and mild forms of diabetes are also seen in this temperament blend.

The phlegmatic-dominant person often complains of lethargy, chronic fatigue, insomnia, frequent headaches, and mild to moderate depression. As mentioned in chapter VI, the phlegmatic-dominant is sensitive to noise and any kind of distraction. For these reasons they avoid crowds and seek solitude. The skin of the phlegmatic-dominant is dry, loose, pale, and subject to irritation and winter itch. Early aging of the skin is notable, and fine wrinkling of the exposed portions of the face and extremities is visible any time past thirty years of age. The subcutaneous fat layer is thin, and it is not unusual to observe visible, dilated blood vessels, especially around the temples and on the backs of the hands. The hands and feet generally feel cold, with a tendency to appear congested with a purplish red hue.

Draper observed a remarkable immunity to all forms of diseases among the phlegmatic person. He observed that cancer is rare in the pronounced phlegmatic person. It is notable that there has never been a serious study concerning the relationship between cancer and constitution. Such a scientific study would be an excellent contribution to medical research.

During middle age, the phlegmatic-dominant tends to have increasing joint discomfort, but rarely shows signs of rheumatoid arthritis or other autoimmune diseases. They will occasionally have urological (especially prostate), kidney, and gastrointestinal disorders. Draper associated the peptic ulcer type as being typically phlegmatic. They require food more frequently than the other temperaments and tend to favor meats over roughage, fruits, and vegetables. Bryant, a famous pathologist, while reporting on autopsies, stated the phlegmatic (ectomorph) type was primarily carnivorous, with small intestines measuring ten to fifteen feet as opposed to the melancholic (endomorph) type, which was primarily herbivorous, with small intestines measuring twenty-five to thirty feet in length. The predominance of absorption function in the melancholic is probably a major factor in their obesity, while the opposite is true in the phlegmatic.

Premature aging becomes increasingly evident after the age of sixty. Kyphosis is a condition of the spinal vertebrae in which changes in the cartilage of the vertebrae causes a humpback. It is usually asymptomatic and worsens with age. Muscular weakness occurs consistent with diminishing sex hormone production. An early senile change of the skin becomes pronounced, along with apparent changes in the central nervous system. As all people age, the number of nerve cells in the brain decreases, nerve impulses become slower, and, consequently, reaction time and performance of tasks become progressively slower. Chronic dizziness, benign positional vertigo, and insomnia are common symptoms of the aging phlegmatic. There is a question as to whether a progressive dementing condition such as Alzheimer's disease and Parkinson's disease is more prevalent in the phlegmatic-dominant. Macular atrophy is the gradual loss of vision due to the progressive deterioration of the macular area of the retina of the eye. It is becoming more common today with the increasing longevity of the general population, and is particularly more prevalent with earlier development in the phlegmatic-dominant individual. Newer management involving laser therapy and visual aids is showing promising results for this debilitating condition.

The phlegmatic (ectomorph) individual is often identified as the hyperthyroid type, which is identified as appearing nervous, anxious, and usually thin. Past researchers have advanced the theory that the ectomorphs (phlegmatics) were dwellers of the coastal regions of the world where iodine supply is high and where thyroid activity is naturally greater. The overactive pituitary gland in the phlegmatic can produce too much thyroid-stimulating hormone, which in turn causes overproduction of the thyroid hormone. However, this is rarely observed. Further characteristics of the phlegmatic, according to Draper, are as follows: "The epiphysis of long bones remains open longer that the other types and the legs and forearms grow to a relatively greater length. Menses usually starts later in the phlegmatic female. Phlegmatics mature slowly both physically and mentally whereas the sanguine and melancholic are larger children that mature earlier in life."

Draper states that in the incidences of tertiary (late) syphilis, the phlegmatic often manifests tabs dorsalis. This is a progressive disease of the spinal cord that begins gradually, typically with intense, stabbing pain in the legs that occurs irregularly and later leads to unsteady walking.

Kretschmer, in his studies, concluded that the phlegmatic constitution is more subject to respiratory tuberculosis and to schizophrenic psychosis. The frequent occurrence of both conditions in the same individual is well-known in institutional patients.

PART THREE

PRACTICAL APPLICATIONS OF THE TEMPERAMENT THEORY

CHAPTER IX

Uses of the Temperament Theory

Prologue

The primary purpose of learning about the four basic temperaments is to discover your own strengths and weaknesses so that you can take advantage of your strengths and learn to strengthen your weaknesses. This is possible by taking control and balancing out your life. Only then can you fulfill your own destiny with maximum health and happiness. Although environmental factors, such as early home life, training, and education, influence your behavior, temperament is the most important factor, because we inherit characteristics of body, mind, and spirit. All temperaments may be modified for better balance, even though the predisposition to favor behavior of your dominant temperament will escort you through life.

One must understand that personality is the outward expression we portray to others. It is often a façade we use to cover up our weaknesses and the negative aspects of our character. The masking of our true self is done primarily to accomplish what we conceive as necessary for social acceptance. In some people, this masking can lead to severe emotional turmoil. These individuals would benefit greatly by learning to balance their temperament rather than fight it, although it is generally true that as people age, their unfavorable traits become more mellow and, thus, more tolerable.

By discovering your own basic temperament, it becomes easier to decide what vocational opportunities are more suitable, what kind of spouse is likely to make a better partner in marriage, how to improve your self-image and character, how to be more successful in interpersonal relationships, how to manage others, and how to be an effective parent.

All people need to be productive. It is good, healthy, and enriching to perform well in a job. Lack of productivity can lead to an emotional vacuum that can affect one's health and longevity. Lack of productive employment or working in the wrong job is equally damaging to one's well-being. In addition to understanding your temperament, it is important to consider the primary motivation behind your desires to achieve goals in life. For instance, if the desire to be educated or become a doctor or lawyer is motivated primarily to share your God-given talents for the benefit of others, then this desire is good and should be fruitful. On the other hand, if this pursuit is primarily motivated to amass wealth or to control or impress others, then this desire would be self-centered, and would most likely lead to a lowered state of self with disappointments in life. By understanding your own temperament, you can seek work or a profession that fulfills your temperament characteristics.

The following briefly describes vocational aptitudes of the four temperaments.

Choosing the Best Vocation

1. The Choleric ♠

Cholerics excel in leadership, motivation, and productivity. However, they do not particularly like attention to detail, analytical planning, committee meetings, or long-range planning. They are usually not craftsmen, but like to supervise craftsmen and construction work that is productive. Foremen, project supervisors, and land developers are a few careers that would suit the choleric temperament.

Cholerics tend to be adventurous and are inclined to become entrepreneurs in new businesses or projects. After it becomes successful, they are likely to get bored and change direction. Although they prefer to do everything themselves, when they delegate responsibility to other people, they can accomplish an amazing amount of work. The choleric is a great motivator of people by virtue of being self-confident and goal-oriented. These characteristics make them very suitable to be military leaders, sports team captains or coaches, statesmen, politicians, or CEOs.

Their greatest weakness as a leader is that they are difficult to please and tend to treat people harshly and arrogantly. They tend to give little or no approval, encouragement, or compliments to their employees or subordinates for fear it will lead to complacency. They frequently resort to criticism, hoping this will inspire greater cooperation, which, of course, fails.

Cholerics could become dynamic and successful preachers with little emotion, but with strong abilities to teach and lead with conviction, as well as organizational and promotional abilities. Those cholerics in this walk of life usually develop successful ministries.

People with the choleric temperament are known to have a "success tendency," not because they are more intelligent than other temperaments, but because they are strong-willed and determined to succeed in their endeavors where others are more likely to quit.

If you have identified yourself as a choleric-dominant, consider the temperament traits you have, both strengths and weaknesses, when choosing a career.

2. The Sanguine ♥

The primary need of the sanguine in any kind of work is extensive exposure to people. Their chief purpose in life is to make other people happy. They excel in giving help and in uplifting the moods of people while conveying love, compassion, and joy. Because of these positive attributes, they excel in the following positions: salespeople, actors, entertainers, preachers, teachers, masters of ceremony, auctioneers, and physicians and other health providers. For example, they are in demand in the news media, where their natural charisma is an advantage in communication.

They tend to be weak on detail, paperwork, and organization. Their chief weakness is a lack of self-discipline, which unfortunately tends to be the most limiting factor in reaching their potential. They generally become disinterested if there is not instant success in their projects. Once they understand their weaknesses and correct them, there is no limit to the sanguine's potential achievements in life.

Sanguines need to be aware that they will most likely be unhappy in a career that doesn't include having people around them.

3. The Melancholic ♦

Almost any humanitarian vocation that requires perfection, self-sacrifice, and creativity can be performed by the melancholic. They are generally higher in IQ and have a more creative imagination than the other temperaments. Melancholics predominate among the world's leaders in art, music, medicine, inventions, philosophy, theology, and education. Many outstanding geniuses of the world have this temperament. Melancholics do not always enter these professions but may become highly skilled craftsmen that provide a meaningful service to humanity. These service roles range from carpenter, bricklayer, plumber, architect, and interior designer to almost every creative profession. Melancholics may excel in acting and portray any character, after which they will revert back to their usual introverted personality.

Professions that include creativity are a must for the melancholic.

4. The Phlegmatic ♣

The phlegmatic person is noted for patience and gentleness and prefers a routine performance of daily duties. They make excellent teachers because of these qualities, especially when teaching young children. These same attributes also apply to their superior teaching abilities in higher education and in the field of education in general. This includes such positions as school administrators, college department heads, librarians, and counselors. They also excel in engineering that requires planning and calculations. Because phlegmatics usually have mechanical abilities, they are especially qualified as mechanics, tool and die specialists, craftsmen, electricians, computer technicians, and appliance or specialist repairmen. Their diplomatic and gentle nature makes them particularly suited to handling people in leadership positions. They are excellent as foremen, supervisors, and managers of people because of these qualities and their aptitude to bring harmony into a dysfunctional, chaotic group. They are notoriously well organized and prepared, reliable, punctual, and work well under a time schedule. They usually remain with the same organization for most of their working years.

Phlegmatics are very capable of leadership positions, but almost always avoid authoritative responsibilities and rarely seek or volunteer for higher positions. They are more interested in a job that promises little conflict, retirement, and security benefits. They are therefore more attracted to government, military, or institutional careers.

If you have identified yourself as a phlegmatic temperament, you would do well to understand all the nuances of this temperament profile when choosing a career.

Choosing a Mate and the Adjustments of Marriage

When choosing a mate, it is so true that opposites attract. This is a natural subconscious attraction that happens without any previous knowledge of differences in temperament. We are attracted to opposite strengths in each other, seeking to fill the natural weaknesses in our own personalities. It is seldom that two people of the same temperament marry each other, although they may communicate and thoroughly enjoy each other's company. Opposites attract and marry while focusing on their opposite strengths. However, without an understanding of personality differences, in time they will tend to focus on the weaknesses, and marital problems will ensue. When we truly understand that one partner's strengths fill the other's weaknesses, we can be grateful for our differences and stop trying to change the other person. Every couple goes through an adjustment period (which experts say lasts about three years), and that is when opposites focus on each other's weaknesses rather than the positive traits. After three years of marriage, the incidence of divorce falls dramatically, as couples learn to accept each other's temperament.

Typical differences, other than being male or female, are not only physical, but include differences in temperaments. In any field, whether it is electrical, chemical, or physical, negative is never attracted to negative. However, the opposite is almost invariably true, negative is attracted to positive. Consequently, predominantly positive temperaments (choleric, sanguine, and their blends) almost universally marry passive temperaments (melancholic, phlegmatic, and their blends). Frequently, sanguines, who tend to be disorganized and undisciplined, are attracted to melancholics, who are cautious, consistent, and organized.

The melancholic tendency to be rigid and aloof admires the outgoing, uninhibited nature of the sanguine. The goal-oriented and dynamic choleric is often attracted to the peaceful, passive, quiet nature of the phlegmatic. In both examples, the reverse is true as well. However, after the honeymoon, each partner tends to focus on the opposite's weaknesses, and problems tend to occur. The friendly and uninhibited sanguine is also forgetful, disorganized, and unreliable. His melancholic counterpart becomes nitpicking, fault-finding, and critical. The dynamic choleric exhibits anger, cruelty, sarcasm, and bullheadedness, while the calm, cool phlegmatic spouse seems lazy, unmotivated, and stubborn.

The period of adjustment must be endured regardless of the temperaments involved, and this can be more easily achieved by understanding and being tolerant of each other's temperament. Literally, each couple must "change for the better that which can be changed, accept that which cannot be changed, and have the wisdom to know the difference." It is highly possible that most marriages can be saved and be happy by accepting each other's weaknesses as well as strengths. Rather than pursuing divorce, which in most cases is far more painful for the entire family, it is better to seek counseling with one who is familiar with the temperaments and who will guide the couple to proper interpersonal relationships and behavior.

Self-Improvement in the Temperaments

Temperament is an inherited trait, much like your body build, the color of your eyes, and your IQ. It will influence your behavior more than anything else in your life. Lesser influences of behavior are the result of your childhood training, home life, education, and other factors, such as motivation. Your basic temperament cannot be changed, but with an understanding of the imbalances in your temperament, you can learn to work toward emotional stability by strengthening your natural weaknesses and maximizing your strengths. Uncorrected weaknesses generally lead to emotional instability manifested by guilt, fear, emptiness, and confusion without a purpose.

No one is perfectly balanced at all times in all the factors that produce emotional stability. One can strive to maintain a balance, but at times weaknesses rise to the forefront. Knowing how to get back on track depends on understanding your temperament. The primary factors in balancing your temperament are to learn to understand and develop a new life based on values of high states, which are love, joy, peace, patience, goodness, faith, self-control, discipline, and worthiness, also known as the fruit of the spirit. This will be discussed further in forthcoming chapters.

1. The Choleric ♠

Cholerics have much work to do in balancing their temperament. They are weak in many of the high-state values listed above. They have very strong self-discipline, strength, and endurance by nature. The areas of self-discipline refer to a strong will, determination, persistence, and consistent energy. Cholerics are weak in the areas of love and compassion, and generally appear insensitive and underdeveloped emotionally. Although they usually find it difficult to express joy, they can reveal much joy when working toward one of their selected goals. They tend to show a hurried or obsessive force in seeking a goal and also reveal a loss of serenity or sense of peace until their goal is met. In the area of goodness, they may show a lack of kindness by their tendency to be caustic and cutting in their speech. Cholerics are generally weak charitably, but when they direct their energies and interests in new endeavors, they can reveal much goodness in giving of themselves. They often lack humility or modesty, and yet at the same time reveal a positive, self-confident attitude. Self-improvement in the choleric can be realized by toning down their natural haughty, proud spirit. As with each temperament, all areas of the choleric can be modified and balanced for self-improvement if they understand their tendencies.

2. The Sanguine ♥

The sanguine is weak in at least six areas of high-state values. Their strengths are that they are loving, compassionate, joyful, and charitable. They love to do good things for people. They lack, however, the serenity to relax, and have a tendency to be restless and combustible. They have little or no endurance, and often leave projects unfinished. Sanguines are generally kind but lack a gentle nature. They tend to be blunt, loud, and often hurtful in their attempted humor without realizing it.

Sanguines are not meek or modest by any means; they tend to be egocentric and boastful. Faith is not particularly important to them, and they tend to conceal their hidden fears and insecurities. The greatest weaknesses of the sanguine are a lack of self-control and self-discipline, which could lead to their destruction if not improved. Again, all these known weaknesses can be favorably modified by self-knowledge, taking control, and developing a new belief system based on the values of high states.

3. The Melancholic ♦

Melancholics are generally weak in five areas. They are weak in the areas of love and compassion, which is revealed in their tendency to be self-centered, perfectionistic, and impatient with the imperfections and idiosyncrasies of others. They are very weak in the spirit of joy, and their personality is more morose, moody, and complaining. They lack an inner peace and security, and their thoughts usually fluctuate from criticism and condemnation to hostility and revenge, and also to suspicion and fear.

Melancholics must learn to invest their life sacrificially in doing good deeds for other people. By turning away from self-centeredness and directing their energies to acts of kindness to others, they can be fulfilled. They also lack a certain amount of meekness and humility, and reveal a trace of haughtiness in their spirit. Becoming more meek and humble is beneficial in making the melancholic less critical and easier to get along with. Melancholics lack faith and limit themselves by unbelief. They can immobilize themselves by fear (e.g., of the future), but by increasing their faith, they will realize that God is always with them and will supply their every need.

4. The Phlegmatic ♣

Even though they are quiet, kind, gentle, and gracious, phlegmatics, like all temperaments, have weaknesses that need strengthening to balance their lives. They lack a loving and compassionate nature, which produces their weak motivations. Phlegmatics notably lack endurance and tend to procrastinate and quit. They have a propensity to do good deeds and a good job once they do get involved in an assignment. One of the best ways to strengthen their weaknesses is faith to overcome worry and fear. Without faith outside of themselves, they are prone to a lifestyle of increasing passivity, procrastination, self-indulgence, and lack of self-control.

Besides increased faith, the phlegmatic would benefit greatly from friendship with an extroverted temperament, which would stimulate love, compassion, and involvement in activities.

Improvement in Interpersonal Relationships

Many theories of behavior have been promoted in the past several decades. The most effective and enduring ones consisted of a model of four styles of behavior. Each type or style is different in actions, reactions, and responses to the same circumstances. All the different theories of the four behavior types have one thing in common. They describe behavioral types corresponding to the four temperaments of Hippocrates, but using different descriptive terms based on the research of Dr. H. J. Eysenck of England. Eysenck was a well-known and respected expert in industrial sales and management. He was also an advocate of the four-temperament theory ascribed to Hippocrates. Educational and industrial testing services generally use the "Eysenck Personality Inventory," also referred to as the EPI. Personality profile testing is used as an effective method to categorize the dominant behavior or temperament of the individual. Both styles of behavior tests would be practical, effective, and useful in training programs involving any organization. It makes no difference if one uses the names choleric, sanguine, melancholic, and phlegmatic or, correspondingly, driver-sensor, expressive-feeler, analytical-intuitor, and amiable-thinker. The net results are the same. The choleric (driver-sensor) must be in charge, and can run any kind of corporation if given the right kind of personnel. The sanguine (expressive-feeler) makes a good sales manager, personnel director, preacher, teacher, or goodwill ambassador. The melancholic (analytical-intuitor) makes a good advertising executive, public relations director, or head of research—anything that demands creativity, especially in the arts. The phlegmatic (amiable-thinker) is best suited as a finance director, head of an engineering firm, or executive vice president.

All of the temperaments or behavior types are inherited; they can be improved, educated, and refined, but never completely changed. It is of great importance to realize that no one style of behavior is better than another. Each one fits better in different kinds of work. Understanding and using the temperament theory would be of great benefit to business, industry, individuals, and families. Essentially, it would improve communication skills, leadership, performance, team-building, and productivity, as well as avoid interpersonal conflicts.

Understanding Your Child's Temperament

Parents have an important responsibility to teach a child values and morals. This is a natural desire for most parents, even if their own past may have been lacking in these areas. Values and morals are not encoded, and must be taught to children no matter how resistant they may be.

There is not room here to cover this topic adequately; however, basic pertinent information for parents may well be helpful here.

First and foremost, children reveal their predominant temperament soon after infancy. With basic knowledge of their differences, parents can soon discern their predominant nature and raise each child accordingly. It is a common and tragic error to assume a child must follow the characteristics of the parent of the same gender. For example, a choleric father will often be disappointed in a son who may be phlegmatic or melancholic in nature, and may abandon that child emotionally to favor another child who fulfills his preference for image and character. This type of conflict is sensed early in life by the child, and could lead to serious emotional consequences during childhood and even into adulthood. Parents who know their child's predominant temperaments can guide and nurture him or her in needed ways until he or she is ready for self-direction. Educationally, each temperament has different learning styles, and the parent must identify those which the child has in order to minimize friction and maximize the pleasure of learning. In addition, this would create a more harmonious home life for the entire family. Always, in raising children, it is essential that love be expressed not only physically by touching, embracing, and kissing, but also by effective communication. Each child has a personality that needs to be understood. Conversing and listening to the child will give the parent a special insight into the particular temperament needs. The following sections exemplify the predominant temperaments in children.

1. The Choleric Child ♠

A choleric-dominant child, besides having a physically athletic build, will show evidence of being strong-willed, energetic, adventuresome, and impatient. These children reveal early leadership qualities and attempt to control adults through temper tantrums. The choleric-sanguine child may show anger by screaming, kicking, or hitting. The choleric-melancholic child will use more subtle means to draw attention, such as refusing to eat or to go to sleep, or holding his or her breath to gain control. All choleric children must be kept busy with responsibilities, in control of something. This could be a pet, his or her bedroom, a backyard play area—anything that the child is totally in charge of. These children often make quick and competent decisions, and may even outsmart their parents at an early age. It is important that the parents of the choleric child provide healthy situations in which the child can express control while at the same time standing firm and resolute in being the final authority for the proper safety and welfare of their child. Inconsistencies on the parents' part in this regard can be very detrimental to the parent-child relationship and produce problems for the undisciplined child in later life.

2. The Sanguine Child ♥

The sanguine child is characterized by being lively and bright-eyed, by being full of curiosity and laughter, by constantly chattering, and by seeking to be the center of attention. They have many creative and intuitive ideas, although they have a short attention span. In school, they strive to be involved in class activities, productions, and the performing arts, seemingly to avoid academics. Any expression of disappointment or anger from the parent or teacher is a form of rejection to this temperament. The sanguine child has a deep need for social acceptance and seeks popularity. For this reason, he or she tends to go along with the crowd and is especially susceptible to peer pressure. A sanguine-choleric child exhibits a more controlling and organized nature. A sanguine-phlegmatic child enjoys fun, but is less organized and less motivated. They have a greater need for physical affection, but discipline, cleanliness, neatness, and handling money wisely don't come naturally to them. Lack of commitment of the parents can easily lead to irresponsibility and immaturity in the child that may continue into adulthood.

The sanguine child tends to fabricate situations and events for approval or to justify their actions, and may even convince their parents. Parents should praise them for telling the unexaggerated truth. A sanguine child always needs encouragement to reach their greatest potential and does not respond well to criticism. They are always motivated to have fun, win approval, and be part of the gang, and are very sensitive to the slightest possibility of rejection.

3. The Melancholic Child ♦

The melancholic child feels, thinks, reacts to, responds to, and reflects on everything deeply. They have the most creative, genius-prone, sensitive temperament, and have a propensity to withdraw when really wanting to reach out. Any neglect or abuse can damage this temperament, whose nature is gentle, insecure, and easily wounded.

Melancholic children are intelligent, good students with high standards and a deep need for perfection. Melancholic-choleric children are meticulous, more outgoing, and bold in their activities. Melancholic-phlegmatics are not as concerned about things being in order and are less compulsive. They tend to have negative thought patterns, and often refuse to communicate their needs, resulting in hurt feelings. They also internalize their deep need for approval rather than openly seeking it like the sanguine.

Melancholic children should be shielded from traumatic dramas or any TV shows that may produce intense reactions. Their parents should constantly direct their thoughts to the positive rather than the negative, as they are most often perfectionists and terrified of failure. Teaching the melancholic child to communicate needs and feelings is a powerful key to curtail chronic depression and unhappiness.

4. The Phlegmatic Child ♣

Phlegmatic-dominant children are cheerful, easygoing, undemanding, and seldom present a problem for their parents. They entertain themselves easily and require less care to make them happy than children of the other temperaments. They seemingly watch the rest of the world go by, because it requires far less energy than getting involved. Every action is evaluated in terms of how much time and energy it requires. The phlegmatic child finds few activities worth the effort to get involved. Because it allows them to lie down and do nothing, TV viewing is a phlegmatic heaven and can cause laziness.

The phlegmatic is not rebellious but has a quiet will of iron. They may act agreeable but have no intention of complying with the parent's request. They may even lie or shift blame to avoid conflict, contention, or responsibility. Phlegmatics of all ages are good listeners and peacemakers, but are indecisive, lack motivation, and reveal a tendency toward procrastination and inactivity.

Parents of phlegmatic children must encourage activity and discourage laziness and procrastination. They must model affection, unselfishness, responsibility, and charity for their children to emulate.

Parenting Guidelines

In the past, the most popular child-rearing technique was to treat every child the same. Fortunately, we now know that this technique is faulty. With the realization that all children are not the same, do not have the same needs, and therefore do not respond to the same parenting techniques, it is obvious that each child must be treated as an individual according to his or her individual temperament. Also, parents must take time to know their own temperaments as they relate to parenting.

In these next sections, the traits of each temperament as related to parenting are discussed in the hope that parents will acknowledge and work with their own strengths and weaknesses as well as their children's.

1. The Choleric Parent ♠

The natural tendencies of the choleric-dominant parent are to dominate; to openly control in an aggressive, unemotional manner; to be demanding, especially concerning productivity; and to be quick to anger. If not checked, these tendencies can produce feelings of incompetence, worthlessness, and depression in their children. Under the influence of choleric parents, sensitive children can inflate or exaggerate these negative feelings to the point of having suicidal tendencies. The choleric parent must understand their children's traits and take great caution not to constantly injure their child's ego. Instead, this parent needs to spend more fun time with their son or daughter. They need to encourage, inspire, and motivate with more loving care and concern, as well as tone down their critical nature.

2. The Sanguine Parent ♥

Sanguine parents are the most likeable parents. They play easily with their children and their peers and elicit much joy and laughter. Their magnetic personality bubbles with optimism, friendliness, love, and compassion. These features can produce some competitive jealousy in a child if the parent gives too much attention to peers or siblings.

The sanguine parent seeks love, acceptance, and approval, even from children. This causes them to be more permissive and weak-willed in setting standards of behavior and enforcing discipline. Their weak characteristics also include tendencies to be restless, forgetful, late for appointments, disorganized, and impractical. They may avoid the increased demands and responsibility of the growing child, especially during the teenage period. The sanguine-melancholic parent usually meets these demands and responsibilities. The sanguine-choleric parent is more acceptable to older children, because both temperaments have magnetic personalities and the added ability to lead and motivate.

3. The Melancholic Parent ♦

Melancholic-dominant parents are highly motivated to encourage their children toward creative and cultural pursuits, such as music, dancing, drama, and the arts. They set high standards for their children in academic achievement. They are duty-bound, responsible, and attentive to their children, always getting them to their activities, school, and lessons on time. A melancholic parent must be careful not to push too hard for achieving high standards if their child is also melancholic. This may produce a negative reaction in their child, who may fear inadequacy caused by never being able to please their parent.

With some melancholic parents, there is a tendency to subconsciously select one child of the opposite sex to be a special companion. The melancholic parent may even rebuff their spouse for the child, who is more easily molded into his or her image of perfection. The parent may then unintentionally prevent that child from living a normal childhood, promoting an adult world filled with adult problems, pressures, and emotional stresses. The parent may feel the child is receiving special attention and cannot possibly see any future emotional problems. That child, when reaching adulthood, may experience bitterness and anger over a lost childhood and exhibit a negative or resentful attitude toward his or her parents. The melancholic parent, in turn, cannot understand this rebellious attitude "after all the years of love and attention given to that child."

The melancholic parent has frequent episodes of depression and is especially prone to be a self-appointed martyr through self-sacrifice. They may make this obvious by exhorting how much they have done for such little thanks or appreciation in return. On the other hand, the melancholic parent may also not exhort on their self-sacrificing tendency, but quietly do everything for the child without verbalizing the personal cost. In either case, the child feels guilt.

The melancholic, like the choleric, is a controlling parent. They are often described in psychological terms as passive-aggressive in nature. In a quiet way, the melancholic parent can do much damage to their children by mere facial expressions of disapproval and disappointment. This powerful, judgmental, and subtle control can make a child feel guilty, inadequate, and overwhelmed. If these parental tendencies are strong enough, the children in adulthood will generally distance themselves from their home and the melancholic parent.

4. The Phlegmatic Parent ♣

The phlegmatic parent has many favorable attributes in child rearing. They are peace-loving, easygoing, and calm, and they do not get upset easily. They prefer routine in their lives and have a stabilizing influence on their children. They do not like change in routine and environment, and generally do not have much need for creativity. Phlegmatic parents enjoy playing with their children, which is preferred over household duties.

They also exhibit certain weaknesses and deficiencies, as in the other three temperaments. They will often avoid conflict by being permissive and side-stepping important issues. Phlegmatic parents are not prone to be dutiful, responsible, or involved in activities. They may appear weak, lazy, and unconcerned to their children, who may also witness parental conflict over the phlegmatic parent's lack of organization in caring for the home and children. A phlegmatic parent tends to neglect paying bills, making appointments or reservations, returning phone calls, and getting home repairs accomplished. The phlegmatic personality subconsciously evaluates everything on how much energy is needed to accomplish the task at hand, including raising and disciplining their children. They naturally like to escape to the effortless comfort of reading or watching TV. They must make a major effort to correct these weaknesses and drawbacks.

Improper Uses of the Temperament Theory

The temperament theory may seem too simplistic for some people, especially those in the scientific world. However, because of its simplicity, it is the best tool ever devised to reach and help the largest number of people. It can also be abused by those who wish to exploit it for their own personal gain or power.

A person may be wrong in their snap judgment of another person for a number of reasons. One may have two dominant temperaments so evenly matched that it is impossible to conclude any temperament blend. This can occur in up to 20 percent of individuals. In some cases, one temperament may have been become dominant as the result of life's past experiences, to the total exclusion of the other. Observe the following rules to avoid the most common abuses of the temperament theory.

Avoid using the temperament theory to humiliate others by analyzing them with special emphasis on the negative characteristics. This can be especially harmful to children when done by an unwitting parent.

As a rule, one may never analyze a person without permission, and never in the presence of others. You may appear to be entertaining, but in fact, you may also unknowingly be producing emotional pain. People in general do not like to be exposed psychologically, especially in public.

Avoid using your known weaknesses as an excuse for self-indulgence. A sanguine with a tendency for overtalking can face that weakness and develop a quieter spirit. A choleric with a tendency to anger can subdue that weakness and summon a more compassionate nature. A melancholic who is prone to criticizing others and being easily depressed via self-pity can aspire to find love, joy, and peace in life. A phlegmatic who lets life slip by because it takes too much effort to do anything must take positive steps to become more actively involved. In all of the above cases, do not excuse yourself saying, "That's the way I am, and I can't change." What you really mean is that you won't change. If you realize that you can modify your life for a more balanced temperament, you then choose to be a happier, healthier person.

Avoid thinking of others only in the image of their temperaments. You may be wrong in your assessment, and then disregard the whole person while concentrating only on temperament. All people need to receive personal interest, love, and acceptance from their family and friends, regardless of looks, physical characteristics, or temperament. Properly used, the temperament theory has far more advantages than potential dangers. In summary, this theory exposes the fact that everyone has strengths and weaknesses, it allows you to improve your temperament by strengthening your weaknesses, and it makes it easier to understand, accept, and love others for themselves.

PART FOUR

DISCOVER AND BALANCE YOUR TEMPERAMENT

Introduction

The intentions of this book are to gain knowledge of the temperaments and be sufficiently objective to determine your own two most dominant temperaments. You may observe that some features of natural strengths are underutilized, while other strengths are overutilized in your life. An honest evaluation and close attention to your weaknesses can lead you in the right direction to strengthen them. It is important to realize that each of us is unique, and we differ in the degrees of the four temperament components that are inherited. We can only surmise the approximate percentages of the temperament in ourselves or another individual. We must also take into consideration the differences in the sexes, IQ, education, environment, and background, for it is evident that many factors are involved that make up the total you. For these reasons, it is impossible to analyze exactly what priority scale of temperament is present in any one person. However, for all practical purposes, we can be relatively accurate in estimating the approximate percentages of the two most dominant components of temperaments. This is accomplished by analyzing the results of the personality tests and the objective observations of the overt characteristics of oneself or the person studied.

After the discovery of your two most dominant temperament components, you must then take steps to modify and balance your temperament. When the weaknesses are strengthened and the temperament is in balance, it will be almost impossible to detect weaknesses of the original temperaments. The modification in your life may well involve a change in habits and thinking patterns that will affect your whole person—body, mind, and spirit.

The following three chapters will discuss body, mind, and spirit in that order. Body care, discussed in chapter X, involves changes in dietary habits, the promotion of routine and proper exercise, changes in sleeping and rest habits, and general care of the body in harmony with the characteristics of each temperament. This knowledge and practice will be of great benefit in establishing a balance for health.

In chapter XII, mind and its aspects will be discussed. The mind must be reoriented to respect and practice the proven wisdoms and ethics of the ages. These are actual natural laws that are now being rediscovered.

In chapter XII, spiritual aspects that nourish the soul will be addressed. Knowledge and practice of these "fruit of the spirit" can have a great impact on the mind and spirit as a result of a change in attitude and behavior. This positive belief system will give you the spiritual nourishment to improve your life and the lives of those around you.

CHAPTER X

Care of the Body

The care of the body includes diet and nutrition, proper exercises, adequate sleep and rest, and general care of the body. It is of great benefit for our earthly self and eternal spirit to love our body and appreciate it. As 1 Cor. 3:17 states, "If any man defiles the temple of God, him shall God destroy, for the temple of God is holy, which temple you are."

Diet and Nutrition

Each temperament has a special attraction to certain foods and seasonings. This tendency is strong enough at times to suggest a genetic memory in one's makeup. However, cultural influence, tradition, and environment possibly play a large part in dietary customs, especially in childhood. It is shown that choleric persons have a natural desire for meat, salt, and alcohol, all of which are known to stimulate their hot, dry choleric nature. The sanguine has a natural preference for creamy, spicy foods and shellfish, which stimulate the hot, wet nature of the sanguine. The melancholic will gravitate to starchy foods, such as breads, pasta, chocolate, cookies, and other pastries, and to caffeine and salty snacks, all of which stimulate their natural melancholic strengths. Phlegmatics prefer frequent snacks consisting primarily of milk, yogurt, cheese, and fruits. A favorite is any of these foods with cookies, which seems to satisfy their low-key, cold, wet, phlegmatic nature.

In all the temperaments, a nutritional diet is necessary to achieve and maintain balance. There is a growing awareness that the correct choice of food we eat plays an important role in our general health and well-being, and in prevention of disease. A nutritional specialist analyzes the health benefits in the body of hundreds of food substances. This is an important consideration in the total care of the patient called holistic medicine. Certain foods have been proven to have anticancer, anti–heart disease, and antiaging properties, and boosting effects on the immune system for protection against infectious and contagious diseases. In general, most of the benefits of food substances are found in fruits, vegetables, whole grains, and legumes. Dairy products, such as milk, butter, cheeses, and eggs, along with poultry, seafood, and meats, are all healthy and wholesome foods that provide adequate proteins and fats in our diet. In each individual there are preferences, likes, and dislikes in food. There are those who are allergic or have intolerances to certain foods.

For health and longevity, it is necessary for all temperaments to limit or eliminate the following: processed foods that are high in sugar and white flour content, especially bakery foods, such as cakes, pies, doughnuts, bagels, cookies, white bread, and other breads that are not whole grain; and excess ingredients, including salt, MSG, and other preservatives, and caffeine. The ingestion of alcohol must be moderated, limited, or eliminated. Favorable liquids for health include fruit juices, green tea, or plain water with or without the addition of lemon, lime, vinegar, or honey. Heavier meals should be eaten earlier in the day or evening, and late-night dining or eating before bedtime should be avoided. A good rule of thumb is to avoid the five whites in excess: salt, sugar, white flour, pasta, and alcohol. French fries or mashed potatoes with gravy, although popular, are not as favorable for health and proper nutrition as the whole potato baked or boiled.

The dietary concepts discussed are generally well-known, but the advent of fast and prepared foods is a large factor, inducing obesity in our hurried society.

Exercise and Physical Activity

Exercise and physical activities are important to all the temperaments. However, there is a difference in the needs and types of exercise and physical activities of each temperament. The choleric-dominant persons need exercise to sublimate and subdue the excess energies and the disposition toward competition in their work. Excellent ways to meet this need include healthy recreational activities, such as athletic competition in racquetball, golf, tennis, or any challenging sport. Aerobics and dancing are also excellent outlets.

Sanguines are more inclined to set their own goals, competing with themselves rather than actively competing with others. They enjoy such exercise as nature walks and outdoor recreation that is not strenuous. Some team games and individual workouts, such as swimming and gymnastics, are healthy stimulants for the components of this temperament.

The melancholic-dominant person is very physical and enjoys vigorous exercises, especially those that require a change of effort, position, and pace. Exercise or some form of physical outlet is needed and important in keeping the earthy melancholic in balance. If physical activity is avoided or lacking, the melancholic will soon become unbalanced and reveal negative characteristics. They become angry and concerned about the imperfections in life, and become very critical of other people, politics, military situations, the economy, the weather, and so on. By nature, the melancholic is passive and generally does not participate in competitive sports. They love to be outdoors in the sunlight when the weather is favorable. They, however, react unfavorably during cold, humid, overcast days when there is a drop in barometric pressure below 30. This situation can have a drastic adverse effect on their mercurial mood swings. A vacation during the winter months to a warm, moist climate is beneficial to balance out their cold, dry nature. They generally prefer ceiling fans rather than air-conditioning during hot, humid weather.

The phlegmatic-dominant person usually prefers a regular routine of mild exercise to maintain a good balance and overcome the tendency to be sluggish. Walking, light jogging, and swimming are recommended and suit their needs. The phlegmatic may enjoy some activities in competitive sports, such as golf and tennis, but, as a rule, they are not attracted to competition in sports. Exercise should be fun and relaxing for the phlegmatic.

Sleep and Rest Habits

In chapter VII, sleep patterns in the various temperaments were discussed in relation to circadian rhythm or body clock. To review, the early risers (referred to as larks) represent approximately 25 percent of the population and are primarily choleric-dominant people. The late risers (after 8:00 AM) and late-night sleepers (referred to as owls) represent approximately 25 percent of the population and are primarily sanguine people. The other 50 percent of the population are various combinations of the temperaments that are called switchers, who can adjust to the time schedule of a lark or an owl, depending on their careers, employers, partners, mates, or family life.

Seven to eight hours of sleep per twenty-four-hour period is essential for optimal health and balance. It is estimated that in our hurried, busy modern life, the average individual in the population has a sleep deficit of one to one and a half hours a day, which leads to negative imbalances in the temperaments. The consideration of adequate sleep and rest is very important in caring for your body and maintaining health and balance.

The choleric-dominant person usually gets from five to six hours of sleep each night. They are characteristic of the larks, who generally retire between 9:00 PM and 11:00 PM. They would benefit from increasing their sleeping hours to seven or eight hours each night, and from taking short naps to replenish their adrenal glands more routinely. This is healthier than indulging in alcohol in the early evening, which stimulates the adrenals artificially.

Sanguine-dominant people tend to be night people or owls; they become more alert, productive, and animated later in the day. Their biological clocks are set to be more efficient in the late morning, and their energy progressively increases toward evening and night. This proclivity must be acknowledged and curtailed if the sanguine wishes to get adequate sleep (seven or eight hours) and participate in morning activities, especially with the choleric and phlegmatic, whose biological clocks are set for earlier morning hours. Sanguines generally sleep well, but may not be sleeping deep enough to clear their mind of the day's stresses. Sleep apnea, which entails inability to maintain deep sleep, is more common in the sanguine. Weight loss and/or corrective sleep apparatus (C-PAP) may be necessary to prevent sleep apnea, which generally produces or exaggerates emotional problems, sleep disturbances, daytime fatigue, and many disease states. A good-quality, firm mattress is recommended to assure adequate sleep and relaxing periods of rest.

The melancholic-dominant person must receive adequate restful sleep; this is pertinent to their health. They do better by sleeping earlier at night and not sleeping late in the morning. They need a comfortable warm temperature with humidity in their house for good sleeping and to counter their natural cold feeling and dry skin. They must avoid refined carbohydrates, to which they are attracted, especially at bedtime, so that they will be hungry for a protein-rich breakfast and one or two teaspoons of raw honey in the morning. Also, a cup of yogurt or warm milk at bedtime will help them to fall asleep quickly. They desire and require warm night clothing and bedding for adequate sleep.

The phlegmatic-dominant person generally requires more sleep than the other temperaments, and the timing should be regular. They need lots of sleep to rejuvenate their lethargic system and thereby boost up their energy to meet the day's activities. A healthy routine of exercise during the day assures them of a stronger desire for a deep and restful night's sleep.

General Care of the Body

Certainly, body hygiene and general care of the body are a given consideration in our modern world. These considerations involve caring for the body by protection from the deleterious environmental effects outside the body and prevention of toxic effects in the body. The harmful effects of environment may include pollution of the water, land, and air, all of which are now becoming a major concern. The prevention of toxic substances in our bodies entails the conscious effort to eliminate poisonous or addictive substances from our diets and lifestyles, the avoidance of unnatural foods, and the removal of any foreign bodies or foci of infection that challenge our immune system. A favorable environment for the body externally will differ to some extent among the four temperaments

Choleric-dominant people are characterized by having a hot, dry nature. They will receive a relaxing and calming effect by cooling the body internally and externally. Their natural desire for meats, salt, and alcohol stimulate their hot, dry nature. They will benefit by favoring the cooling effects of such foods as dairy products (eggs, milk, and cheese), oatmeal, fruit, and vegetables. Vegetables are basically disliked or rejected by the choleric, but such foods will have a cooling, hydrating, and calming effect on the choleric nature. Externally, their hot, dry nature will benefit from frequent warm showers followed by the application of a cooling, lubricating lotion. For vacation, they usually enjoy the cooler climates and particularly winter sports, such as tobogganing, skiing, and snowmobiling, all of which are advantageous to the choleric.

The sanguine-dominant has a natural constitution that is characterized by being hot, wet, and restless. Frequent drinking of cool water is beneficial in reducing body heat. Short showers every morning will boost the sanguine's positive characteristics, especially when the water temperature is quickly changed from hot to cold. A hot shower or sauna followed by rolling into winter snow can also have an exhilarating effect. Ceiling fans or air-conditioning has a calming effect on the hot, wet nature of the sanguine, who tends to perspire easily during warm, humid weather.

The melancholic-dominant has a natural constitution that tends to be cold and dry. They benefit from long warm showers or baths, which warm their body and hydrate their dry skin. The short warm shower may not be sufficient to warm their body, and in fact may tend to stimulate the melancholic temperament and induce an imbalance. Applying a lubricating lotion after the shower or bath helps maintain the moisturizing effects of the water.

The phlegmatic-dominant temperament naturally tends to be cold and wet. In general, anything that cools their body internally or externally may be detrimental and tends to create an imbalance. They should avoid cold drinks, especially frequent snacks of cold milk and cookies. Short warm showers and baths are beneficial in warming their bodies. It is advisable for them to take vacations, especially during the winter months, in warm, dry places, such as islands or deserts.

Care of the body involves several modalities of treatment that are becoming more popular and in demand, including massage, physical or spa therapy, yoga, and music therapy. The importance of these alternative methods of therapy is being recognized and incorporated into modern medicine. This subject will be further discussed in the chapter on holistic medicine.

CHAPTER XI

Mind Reorientation, Laws of Ethics, and Wisdom

Mind Reorientation

Awareness of and obedience to the laws of ethics and wisdom are necessary to achieve a balance in your temperament. In recent years, a cellular biologist, Dr. Bruce Lipton, proved scientifically in laboratory research that behavior of living cells is not determined by the DNA in the cellular nucleus, as was originally thought. Behavior was discovered to be ruled entirely by a belief system that affects the cellular membrane, which is the true brain of the cell. The mind can therefore be reoriented and reprogrammed to replace the negative, wrong, and harmful information stored in the subconscious mind. Reorienting your subconscious mind with positive thoughts, ethics, and wisdom will favorably change your reactions to life's experiences.

This revolutionary discovery by Dr. Lipton will eventually change the course of research in biology and medicine. It will, in effect, negate many of the present concepts in psychology and biology, as represented by the Newtonian theory and Darwinism. It will downplay the mechanical theory and physics of man in favor of Einstein's quantum theory of energy in living cells. The in-depth discussion of these revolutionary changes is beyond the scope of this book, but nevertheless, must be addressed.

We will now acknowledge some of the important laws of ethics and wisdom that will favorably change your thinking pattern to achieve desirable high states of self. It has been said that there is no such thing in life as *always* or *never*. However, there are rules revealed in ethics and wisdom that have proven to be true in the vast majority of instances. All people have imprinted in their subconscious minds negative thoughts that were instilled in early childhood. These negative thoughts come from generational, parental, traditional, and environmental influences. The subsequent behavior pattern is not determined by heredity but by these worldly influences that can induce low states of mind, which are detrimental and often outmoded. It is important to understand these mental mechanisms in order to change one's thinking pattern toward the positive high states of mind. Laws of ethics and wisdom and described in the following section.

Natural Laws of Ethics and Wisdom

1. The Law of Meditation

Patanjali was a Hindu mystic who lived in India in the first to third centuries BC and is considered to be the person who established the tradition of meditation. Many consider his words on meditation as methods to know God and to achieve a heightened level of awareness (a high state of mind and self).

Meditation should be practiced at least once daily in a quiet, relaxed, private environment without distractions. This is reflected in the Bible in Psalm 46:14: "Be still and know that I am God." The principal reason to meditate is out of one's desire to make a conscious contact with God. By practicing meditation, we can contact the power of our source, awaken our own creative energies, and realize our desires and goals. Concentration and dialogue with your higher source expressing gratitude, love, guidance, and the higher spiritual values will prove of great benefit. Mere words without substance would obviously be meaningless and unfruitful. An excellent time to meditate is early in the morning at sunrise, or in the evening at sundown. The time spent may vary from a few moments to an hour, and the subject of meditation may be an event, need, guidance, or organized prayer. The methods of how to meditate are available in many instructional books or through classes. However, it is the quality and substance of meditation that are important.

Meditation can clear the subconscious of negative thoughts by concentrating on the positive affirmations of the high states of self. The use of these affirmations along with visualization (especially with the color purple), repetitive prayer, and the power of sound, such as the spoken word, mantras, and background classical music, can produce proven beneficial effects on the body. Physiological changes include reduced heart rate, reduction in high blood pressure, lowered stress, slowed metabolism, and increased immunity.

Access to the Divine intelligence through meditation does not require higher education or an exceptional intellect. In fact, overeducation may be a breeding ground for disbelief and pride. Those who try to seek the truth by means of intellect alone become lost and stray farther away from it. However, those who meditate with intuitive listening and a stilled mind can receive answers and guidance to obtain their desired goals in life if they are prepared to receive them. It is important that certain sacred messages and spiritual experiences be kept secret from your friends and even your closest companions. Telling others all that is gained in meditation could block the recipient from receiving further gains from meditation.

It has been said and proven that people who meditate and actively embrace thoughts of high-state values are rewarded in all aspects of life. They experience better relationships with people, superior results in finance, good health, and good luck, and often avoid premature aging and death. They are blessed with longer lifespans, more positive relationships, wonderful children, thrills, laughter, and sounder sleep. They are imbued with self-knowledge, self-control, confidence, high self-esteem, and contentment in their lives. On the other hand, people preoccupied with ego-induced and worldly low-state values exhibit hate, greed, envy, jealousy, revenge, and other low-state values. They are penalized by experiencing chronic and life-threatening health problems, conditions that are treatable but not cured (migraine headaches, insomnia, asthma, backaches, certain cancers, etc.). Such people usually reveal weak immune systems and suffer from chronic fatigue or depression. They frequently experience bad luck, have disappointing children, and have self-destructive habits, such as gambling, drug abuse, and a secret desire to lose, as well as feelings of helplessness, and may even harbor a death wish.

Occurrence of heart attacks and strokes is known to increase during the early morning hours, when one is likely to awaken with negative and stressful thoughts. Positive meditation would be especially beneficial at that time in reducing and preventing these life-threatening situations.

2. The Power of Prayer

Prayer may involve many intentions including desire, wishes, and intercessions. Throughout the ages, prudent wisdom and spiritual philosophies have reiterated that there is a time to be born, and a time to die. Birth and death would appear to be the domain of our creator, and according to his will. The time to live, however, gives mankind a choice. This choice is between any adherence to the high states of self and the known spiritual laws, and the choice to be self-dominated by pride and ego. The former choice includes Christ's statement, "Ask and you shall receive." This implies that through belief and faith in your creator, you can have abundance with long life, health, and happiness, until the time of your death. Adherence to high states gives purpose and credibility to a general correlation between our physical and spiritual states and the power of prayer. The meaning of disease may be hidden and unknown to us—secretly known only to the Divine. It is wrong to attribute bad health, illness, or physical debilitation to any spiritual shortcomings to God. In any given case, we simply may not know why serious illness or physical disability occurs. This is a mystery and apparently is beyond any human understanding.

Prayer can be an effective mode of therapy, which, unfortunately, has been rejected by modern medical education, which regards it as unscientific. It is now becoming more possible to allow science and spirituality to be complementary to each other. Dr. Larry Dossey, in his excellent book *Healing Words,* discusses at length all aspects of prayer and the scientific literature investigating the subject. He found that more than half of the reports were conducted under stringent scientific laboratory conditions and revealed that prayer brought about significant changes in a variety of living beings, from bacteria to humans. He concluded that this body of knowledge was ignored as if it did not exist because it did not fit the prevalent scientific thinking. He discovered that prayer could be effective regardless of distance or any barrier, whether physical or electromagnetic. Because of the sensitive, personal nature of the subject, Dr. Dossey feels that prayer as a therapy should not be suggested unless the patient brings up the subject. In this case, he feels it would be wise to suggest counseling with a priest, minister, rabbi, or someone schooled in the patient's faith.

The subject of the power of prayer reminds me of a particular incident that occurred in my practice several years ago. On a dermatologic consultation I was asked by a surgeon for my diagnostic opinion and treatment recommendation on a possible melanoma on a woman's left breast. The lesion was a rapidly enlarging blue to red nodule almost 1 cm in diameter, which clinically suggested a malignant melanoma. A sunburst discoloration surrounded the lesion for several centimeters, and there was an associated left axillary lymph node enlargement and tenderness. Three reported biopsies, one involving the central lesion and two involving the sunburst area, all revealed the most lethal type of malignant melanoma, grade four. I reported that surgery would be futile at this stage, because there was also clinical evidence of left axillary metastasis. The humble patient and her daughter were consoled, and I suggested that she live out her life graciously. She responded that she would, with prayer.

Ten years later, the daughter appeared in my office as a patient, and I gave mention and condolences on her long-departed mother. The daughter promptly replied, "Oh, Mother is fine. She is in the waiting room." I immediately asked for permission to reexamine her mother without charge, and this was granted. To my astonishment, there was no evidence of any preexisting melanoma or sunburst. Follow-up chest X-rays were normal, and there was no left axillary enlargement of lymph nodes. This woman was apparently cured of her melanoma and appeared in be in good health.

I reported this case orally at a dermatology meeting, but without any follow-up written report. I suggested that this case resembled a few other similar cases in the literature of spontaneous self-healing, most likely on the basis of immunity buildup from the invading malignant cells. The power of prayer was never mentioned. To this day I cannot prove in which manner the body healed itself, but I am more inclined to believe that prayer may have been the primary healing factor in this case.

3. The Law of Truth

"And you shall know the truth and the truth shall set you free," states John 8:32.

One must always speak the truth, even if it hurts. The high state of truth can cure depression, rationalization, denial, overcompensation, and defensiveness. Truth will always prevail, and leads to completion of one's purpose in life. Liars, or low-state people, may mask the truth temporarily, but are eventually defeated by forgetting their lies, aborting successful relationships and producing unhappiness in them. Everybody has lied on occasion, mainly to avoid hurting someone's feelings. These "little white lies" may be understandable and even permissible at times if it is not hurtful to anyone. However, if lying is an ongoing practice, it can lead to a low state of mind, with unfavorable consequences.

Being truthful and supporting those who are truthful can have a profound beneficial effect in building national unity. Children and adults tend to imitate those whom they look up to and respect. We all are a role model for someone. A truthful nature is revealed in our speech pattern by what we don't say, what we do say, and how we say it.

John Keats (1795–1821), a famous English poet, concludes in the poem *Ode on a Grecian Urn*, "Beauty is truth, truth beauty. That is all ye know on earth and all ye need to know." His lines of poetry tell us to know our truth and follow our hearts, and we will see beauty everywhere. This characterizes the high state of self observed in fully functioning people.

4. The Law of Attraction

- You receive what you believe.
- As a man thinks, so shall he be.
- You receive by giving.
- What goes around comes around.
- You reap what you sow.
- Do unto others as you would have them do unto you (the golden rule).

These are all true statements that reveal a basic spiritual law of the universe, known as the law of attraction, also called the law of the circle, or karma. High states beget high states and low states beget low states. In other words, you receive what you believe, whether you want it or not. If a person harbors thoughts of high states, such as love, joy, peace, and patience, he or she will in turn receive like rewards. On the other hand, if one harbors thoughts of low states, such as hate, envy, jealousy, and revenge, such a person will receive the same or like experiences. Thinking and believing in abundance will produce abundance, whereas thinking and believing in scarcity and poverty will produce scarcity and poverty. A basic principle of abundance is "you receive by giving." The greatest gift to others is sharing your personal endowed talents and special qualities that deliver love, comfort, and joy.

5. The Law of Voluntary and Independent Service

The practice of this law is rewarded with high states of positive returns. The very act of giving voluntary, independent, charitable, and personal services induces others to follow suit. This type of service satisfies a deep need to contribute to the world and is rewarded by feelings of well-being, belonging, and receiving approval without seeking or needing these feelings. Generosity (or charity) is a high state; those who are stingy, selfish, and cheap are in a low state. Their selfishness usually activates a paradox of irony whereby they may chase a penny and lose a dollar. Generous people who also give of themselves will usually make more money and have abundance.

6. The Law of Keeping Commitments

The keeping of agreements and being responsible for your own actions creates a high state of mind. It is crucial in developing trust of others. It goes hand-in-hand with truth and leads to completion of one's purpose in life. Breaking agreements and appointments, making up excuses, being untruthful, and not taking personal responsibility for your actions produces a low state of mind, with unfavorable consequences. The excessive need to be right and the use of excuses to complain and blame others for their lot in life also produces a low state of mind. This low state fortifies that great need to be right and justifies the person's negativism, including continuously making mistakes, using poor judgment, and having neurotic tendencies.

7. The Law of Acceptance and Forgiveness

A high state of mind occurs when we accept things as they are and forgive past injuries. All we really have is the now. The past is history and cannot be undone, and the future is unknown. The present is truly a present or gift to be accepted graciously and with gratitude. We all must learn and grow from the problems we face now. We must accept and love ourselves as we choose to be now. One of the greatest illusions of mind believes that the past is responsible for present conditions in our lives. Everyone can blame past conditions or experiences and use them as excuses for our shortcomings, failures, and inaction. A simple truth is that the past is over and cannot be recalled. Learn from it, but do not loiter in the past or try to dwell in the future. Preoccupation with experiences of the past and expectations of the future will prevent you from fully living in the present. We can only live and make choices in the now. It is important to live each moment of the present in a high state of self.

Forgiveness is the antidote to the poisons of low-state bitterness and hatred that you may retain long after the initial hurt. If that poisonous venom is not removed, it can destroy your peace of mind and, eventually, your meaning and purpose in life. Forgiveness also involves self, and it is often harder to forgive ourselves than to forgive others. Guilt occurs as a result of committing an infraction or an offense. Guilt is a low state, which can depress the spirit and all of life's forces. Confessing, repenting, and asking God's forgiveness is necessary to resolve the guilt. Forgiveness can produce immediate results of high states with love, joy, compassion, peace of mind, and a sense of meaning and purpose in life.

8. The Law of Moderation

"Everything in moderation" is an ancient Greek proclamation of wisdom. Overworking of a natural strength and overpowering actions in any situation can, in fact, invoke a paradox of inhibition and rejection in reaching a goal. If one is too overzealous or forceful in pursuing a goal, it is apt to repel the very person or situation necessary to accomplish that goal. For example, if the pursuit of a mate is too aggressive, roughshod, and demanding, a rejection is more likely to occur. This paradoxical rule applies to any situation in life, even when the involved person is righteous. It occurs whenever one is overcontrolling, overcondemning, overselling, overzealous, or overneedy. A common theme in many modern songs is the overneeding of a personal love. It is natural to want and pursue a personal love. However, we only need the true source of love, which is the love of God.

9. The Law of Respect, Gratitude, and Appreciation

A component of a high state is respect for others, especially for your elders and your own parents. This respect leads to other components of high states, such as gratitude and appreciation for the gifts of life. One must respect, honor, and be grateful to your parents, who were instruments in giving you life and did their best for you under the circumstances of their lives. You may differ from your parents in philosophy and in how you raise your own children, but taking responsibility in sharing this wisdom with your children is a high state in itself. The wisdom of respect, gratitude, and appreciation is not genetically encoded, and when expressed, not only extends to and includes God, but also to healing and completion of life's purpose. When it is not expressed, it can lead to a low state of depression, regret, and a loss of fulfillment, meaning, and purpose in life.

Respect includes the traditional wisdom of civility, which has been taught through generations since antiquity. These are mannerisms that elicit politeness and courtesies in the daily encounters with other people. They are positive, promote fellowship with ease of communication, and lead to high states of respect in ourselves and others. Strictly speaking, these mannerisms are not laws, but they do resemble the commandments of Moses by emphasizing the "thou shalt not." For example, in the presence of others, one should not sing or hum to oneself, drum one's fingers or feet, speak or whisper when others speak, sit while others stand, walk while others stop, be a flatterer, nor hastily believe idle gossip. "Silence is golden," except when you have something to add to a conversation. Right speech is truthful, supportive, kind, and respectful. It is short, comprehensive, and never exaggerates, which is really akin to lying. Right speech also means to overcome passivity, speak at the right time, and stand up for what you believe is right regardless of what others think.

Restructuring the Subconscious Mind

The subconscious mind has stored in it many more millions of facts and concepts of life than the conscious mind. It is the part of one's mind that automatically recalls and performs all learned facts, concepts, and natural instincts. To my knowledge, investigators generally believe that experiences in prebirth life in the womb could influence the long-term behavioral health of the individual. The prevalent concept is that genetics dominate all behavior and characteristics of the individual, and genetics also accounts for the differences between siblings without any influence of the parents. The true reality is that parents have overwhelming influence on the mental and physical attributes of the children they raise. This is true during both pre- and postbirth periods, and high-state environmental conditions provided by the parents can optimize the genetic and physiological development of the child.

Genetic imprints are responsible for the instinctual behavior of lower animal life and are necessary for survival, which includes the need for food and shelter. Humans do not have instincts that automatically protect us and help us find food and shelter. We have a choice in these matters, whereas lower animals do not. Certain behavioral instincts, however, are innate in human nature, such as the suckling instinct in infants, their quick movements away from fire, and their automatic ability to swim moments after birth. The body's physiological mechanisms are genetically programmed instincts; these include heart rate, blood pressure, blood flow, bleeding or clotting time, and body temperature. However, even these instincts can be consciously modified by biofeedback and focused control. In humans, the fundamental behavior, beliefs, and attitudes stored in the subconscious mind primarily arise before the age of six from their parents and by observing their environment. Parents and environment in turn are influenced not only by genetics, but by factors that were traditional, generational, and cultural. These beliefs are registered in the subconscious mind as absolute and true facts. The conscious mind in later life develops enough to critically assess parental pronouncements. However, once these beliefs are programmed in the subconscious mind, they are also registered as truths and facts. This programming unconsciously determines the behavior and potential of the individual throughout life. Information stored that comprises negative low states is detrimental and of no value to one's future life. The sum of the genetic imprint of our basic temperament and the innate instincts, in addition to the beliefs we learn from our parents and the environment, collectively form the subconscious mind. Removal of the harmful negative low state can favorably affect health, longevity, purpose, and happiness in life. This can be accomplished by proper psychological counseling, instilling values of the high states of mind, spiritual awakening, and daily meditation.

CHAPTER XII

Spiritual Values and the High States of Self

Spiritual values and the high states of self are actually dominant thoughts in the mind. These thoughts are high-frequency energy vibrations that are in harmony with the high-state vibrations of the universal mind. The universal mind (also known as the universal intelligence source, nature, Holy Spirit, God, etc.) recognizes only good or positive values and will only return the like—good or positive values—back to the sender. You receive what you think and believe.

This law of attraction has been known throughout the world since antiquity, and is revealed as wisdom. All great philosophies and religions understood and expounded on these principles. Wayne W. Dyer, in his book *Wisdom of the Age,* affirms that these principles are essential for health and balance in life. The basic teachings of all religions, including Buddhism, Taoism, Judaism, Islam, and Christianity, are in harmony with the belief in natural law and Divine intervention. The administration of these religions may in fact be, at times, corrupt or detrimental to humanity due to the egos or power-driven philosophies of worldly men. Nevertheless, the truths of these good and positive values were reflected in the philosophies of the American Indians and of great spiritual leaders of the past, such as Confucius, Pantanjali, Mahatma Gandhi, St. Francis of Assisi, and Mother Teresa.

The spiritual values and high states of self are elaborated under the following nine headings: love, joy, peace, patience, goodness, gentleness, humility, faith, and self-control. (These spiritual values are also known as "fruit of the spirit" in the biblical verse Galatians 5:22–23.) At the end of this chapter is a chart of the nine headings summarizing the meaning of each value (Chart 9). Finally, a short review of the negative or low states of mind that exist in worldly and ego-based people is presented for comparison of the effects on the whole person (Chart 10). This presentation of the high states will start with love.

High States of Self

1. Love
Hatred stirs up strife, but love covers all transgression. —Proverbs 10:12

The most powerfully important, and essentially all-inclusive, spiritual value is love. Love is said to be the universal source that governs all spiritual laws and maintains high states of self. Love must be unconditional to include all things of the planet (earth, water, sky, all living forms, and humanity) and also the universe (sun, moon, stars, and all things seen and unseen). Love nullifies all negative thoughts and images. It is purpose-driven and leads to freedom from all ego-induced low states of mind, which are negative emotions, such as hate, fear, guilt, envy, jealousy, sadness, doubt, anger, suffering, pain, and disease. These low states of self are slow vibrational energies that emanate from man's ego. They are subject, however, to the universal law of attraction which returns like emotions (i.e., hate begets hate, fear begets fear, etc.). The universal mind does not recognize nor emanate these low vibrational energies. However, it does not prevent these emotions from occurring, and such negative values are based on man's own ego and choice. Research at the Institution of Heart Math has shown that love enhances immunity and improves hormonal balance in the body. Conversely, low-state emotions, such as anger, fear, and frustration, have the opposite damaging effects on the body organs and the immune system.

William Butler Yeats writes in a poem of "Soul Love" (taken from Dr. Wayne W. Dyer's book *Wisdom of the Ages*), which says the truest test of love has nothing to do with external appearances, but is for you alone. He suggests letting the soul of those you love receive your attention, and to love yourself as God does, for yourself alone. Look past the indicators of aging and into the part of yourself that has never aged and never will.

In my practice of dermatology, I would frequently encounter elderly patients who wanted to know the diagnosis of the dark age spots notable on the face. Though I knew these spots were benign, rather than giving a medical opinion, I often responded with, "Sir, they are badges of wisdom," or "Dear lady, they are only delayed beauty marks."

We must ignore the incessant propaganda that encourages us to hang onto eternal youth and instead love ourselves not for our looks, but for our character and soul. When expressing love to others, emphasize what you truly love about them, rather than how they happen to look. Talk to their eternal soul rather than the garage that houses it.

In essence, the two all-encompassing commandments of Christ cover all aspects of love when He commands us to do the following:

- Love your God with all your heart, soul, mind and strength.
- Love your neighbor as yourself.

Loving God includes all of his creations, seen and unseen, including those in the water, land, and sky, and including the entire universe, the sun, the moon, and the stars. We must always be thankful for the interrelated functions of all his creations, for the benefits to mankind, nature, and the world. It would seem impossible and unreasonable to think that these complex and perfect creations and functions exist without the presence and guidance of a universal intelligence. We must accept all of these gifts with gratitude, love, and faith.

To love your neighbor as yourself certainly implies that you cannot love your neighbor unless you love yourself first. "Yourself" represents your body, mind, and spirit, which are all divine gifts from your creator and must be treated with care, respect, gratitude, and love. The golden rule evolved from this commandment: "Do unto others as you would have them do unto you."

Pierre Teilhard de Chardin (1881–1955) was a French-born Jesuit priest who proclaimed that love is the most powerful energy, which he called the universal synthesizer. He suggests that love will eventually link and draw together all elements of the world and humanity toward a spiritual unity.

I once read a beautiful essay on first and last love by C. S. Lewis in *Readings from Meditation and Reflections,* and I wish to share his sentiments. First and last love is a continuing spiritual experience that lingers in everyone's life, yet is rarely mentioned. At an early age we all experience a profound sense of love that we immediately attribute to and focus on one individual. These feelings are deep, with desires and passion that we always remember and that last throughout life. However, they are really never realized, never quite fulfilled, and fade like dying echoes. It is kept a secret in our heart and soul, and was something that existed before we met our spouse or our friends, or chose our work in life. It is God, who is our first love, who lingers in our heart even unto the last breath when our consciousness is lost to everyone else. He is the first and last love who will prepare a place for us in heaven, a place especially made for us. Bishop Sheen in one of his early TV broadcasts reflected this experience when he said that the anticipation of worldly things is great but the realization is not; the anticipation of spiritual things is not but the realization is great.

2. Joy
Our mouth was filled with laughter and our tongue with joyful singing. Then they said among the nations, The Lord has done great things for them.
—*Psalm 126:2*

Joy is a high state of self that produces bliss, harmony, balance, and enlightenment in life. It induces happiness, jubilant thoughts, and enthusiasm. It involves humor and laughter not at the expense of others, but out of self and life's experiences. A sense of humor and laughter are healthy stimulants in all situations of life, even when it seems serious to some others. Seeing things as a whole and as being ridiculous can invoke humor and laughter, but if seen from another angle, some people may take offence, without realizing the hurtful humor was unintentional.

One of my close friends was the late Don Knotts, a celebrity who appeared in *The Andy Griffith Show* and other productions. We grew up together in a small West Virginia town. In spite of the poor economic conditions, we shared many joyous times together with singing, humor, and laughter. Don was always naturally funny, especially with his facial expressions and body language. I remember asking him, "How are you feeling today, Don?" And he responded, "Oh, fine, I guess. Have you heard anything different?" He asked me once to examine his throat, which was sore. After examining it, I said, "Your throat is red and probably sore, but I'm not worried." Don responded, "Gee, thanks. You know, if you had a sore throat, I wouldn't worry either." As I said, we had many laughs, and our friendship doubled the joy and lessened any grief we experienced. I believe God loves humor and laughter, too.

The Jewish prisoners in Nazi war camps owe much of their survival to their great ability to invoke the joy of humor and laughter in those dire circumstances. Joy can come from giving a personal service or a purposeful giving of any natural gift. These natural gifts include musical talent, art, humor, poetry, and all creative works. Joy is the satisfaction that comes from the fulfillment and completion of a committed service to others. Joy is also associated with expressions of gratitude and appreciation for receiving God's gifts that made possible the completion of life's purpose.

Sadness is a low vibrational energy that is the product of the ego. Joy is the spiritual antidote to sadness and is a fast vibrational energy that produces a high state of self. Sadness cannot persist in the presence of joyful thoughts. You have a choice of letting go of sad thoughts and opting for joyful thoughts. Ultimately, this fast vibrational energy of joy will be your natural state—a high state of self. The lives of saints and sages have always exhibited joy, freedom, and a profound feeling of love for every living creature. You, too, can radiate the energy of joy to others who appear to be experiencing sadness and depression. These people may in fact be great teachers in your life. They provide the stimulus to choose joy and peace over depressed states and sadness.

Bringing joy can be a simple act of comforting or giving service in some small way to another person. This joy can come from settling a dispute, telling people you love exactly how you feel about them, asking forgiveness from anyone you have violated or offended, and in general replacing hurt with joy. Dr. Wayne W. Dyer, in his books, advocates the daily practice of meditation for bringing joy to replace sadness. Repeating the thought, "I feel supremely happy," can change your whole body. Thoughts, facial expressions, health, and attitude can quickly move from sadness to joy. George Bernard Shaw (1856–1950) was a dynamic and witty Irish philosopher. He suggested we let go of self-absorption and get involved in the true joy of life, which is to feel you are living with joy for a purpose.

3. Peace
But all who listen to me will live in peace with safety, unafraid of harm.
—*Proverbs 1:53*

Peace is a high state of self that occurs in a mind that is calm, relaxed, serene, and silent. It is said that the language of God is silence that speaks the true meaning of peace. It is "letting go" and surrendering to the higher states of the universal mind. This universal mind and intelligence is God, who is always present in us, at work, at play, and at all times in our lives. He expresses infinite love and offers infinite peace. We can only reach and maintain his peace by retraining our minds to think and accept life as it is rather than as we think it should be. We must use our minds solely for peaceful thoughts rather than occupying our minds with negative thinking or continually looking for occasions to be nonpeaceful. We cannot wait or expect other people or situations to change before we can receive peace. However, if you think in terms of already having peace, then you become a giver of peace and radiate a sense of calmness to everyone you encounter. Then, your presence will sooth any tumultuous situations.

Certain people may easily "push your buttons" and trigger in you feelings of frustration, turmoil, and anger. These people are really master teachers, and usually are those whom you love, or are the closest in your life. Such people may include your spouse, your children, relatives, friends, or associates. These great teachers are continuous reminders, sent by God, to help you to master your self-control and learn the ability to be at peace with yourself at all times. Only then will you be able to radiate outward the peace that is within you and truly become "an instrument of thy peace," as in the prayer of St. Francis of Assisi.

In a recent group discussion on peace, it was humorous to listen to the various descriptions. One person spoke up: "Peace is obtained when the last child leaves home and the dog dies." Another person claimed, "Keeping peace in the family requires patience, love, understanding, and at least two television sets."

God and peace are really synonymous. You can't have peace if you believe you are separate from God and don't need him. Being at peace with yourself allows you to deal with the problems of daily life and gives you an awareness that you are being guided to act reasonably and sensibly. Peace gives you understanding that there are no accidents in life, and that personal spiritual advances are preceded by experiences of adversity or some type of tragedy. We must not harbor any self-repudiating feelings, such as guilt, regret, shame, or blame. Past experiences served a purpose for you to arrive at your present state of spiritual development.

Peace nourishes our souls by allowing them to commune with God. This occurs through love and appreciation of nature, thankfulness, prayer, and meditation. In meditation, we learn to contact the source of our inner peace and gain spiritual insight with self-discovery. The technique of meditation chosen is not as important as the daily practice of meditation. This includes forgiveness for all transgressions of others and of ourselves. Meditation is strongly recommended to obtain balance and a high state of self, which is essential for lasting peace of mind.

If possible, avoid loud, boisterous, and argumentative people, but when among them always choose to have peaceful thoughts. There is a clever analogy: Where there is no God among them, there is no peace. Where there are those who know God, they will know peace.

4. Patience
Be glad for all God is planning for you. Be patient in trouble and always be prayerful. —Romans 12:12

Patience is an enormous virtue and guide in life. It is a high state of self that is sadly lacking in our world today. The secret role of nature is to teach patience, and we must adopt its character to achieve balance. Patience encompasses many related high states, including tolerance, persistence, endurance, and being long-suffering or "waiting for God" to direct you. God, also known as the universal mind, speaks to us through others, young or old, and through daily experiences and intuition. It behooves us to take time to listen, and to practice awareness and objective observation. We must then be patient to understand these messages. Patience and tolerance lead to the acceptance of all humanity, regardless of the differences of beliefs and behaviors. The high state of patience produces confidence, decisiveness with clarity of mind, and a feeling of peace.

Strong will is another aspect of patience. Perseverance results from a strong will, and imparts the staying power necessary to achieve a goal. My mother would say, "Where there is a will, there is a way." She never gave up after my father died at an early age, and she was left to raise and educate eight children and run a family grocery store. All of the children became educated professionals, and she was named Mother of the Year in West Virginia in 1942.

Impatience is a low state of mind that breeds fear, stress, and discouragement. The negative consequences are evident in the natural law of receiving what you give. This negativity is witnessed daily on the highways, in shopping centers, and in virtually all areas of public gatherings. In heavy traffic, we can substitute impatience manifested in anger with the high state of listening to soothing music on the radio. We can also pray that youth will show the same enthusiasm in getting ahead in the world as they often display in traffic. Our speed-driven society is addicted to promises of quick fixes and instant gratification or success in reaching our goals. The ego-driven person displays impatience with those who do not talk, move, eat, or drive fast enough to suit them. Listening to one's ego is a learned response, which can be a killer in many ways and is manifested by impatience. However, the future can gradually become brighter and more beautiful when we decide to renew our lives and follow the knowledge of ancient wisdom in the image of our creator. The truth is, there is no shortcut to maturity; only patience produces results.

Ancient wisdom and biblical revelations teach that all good things in life come with patience in harmony with nature—slowly, steadily, and surely. Confucius (551–479 BC) wrote about the folly of impatience. His lesson teaches that mankind must learn from his own nature that the healing process proceeds precisely at its own pace, regardless of a desire to fix it quickly. Shakespeare shared this wisdom when he wrote, "How poor are they that have not patience? What wound did ever heal but by degrees?" Patience is the key ingredient in all functions of the natural world. If we try to speed up and interfere with the pace and process of nature, we are likely to encounter dissatisfactions or complications. Such examples are seen in trying to ripen fruit quickly, interfering with plant life before maturity, inducing labor in pregnancy prematurely, or interfering with the growth and maturity of any natural process. "Everything on earth has its own time and its own season," as it says in Ecclesiastes 3:1.

5. Goodness
It is more blessed to give than to receive. —Acts 20:55

Goodness is a high state of self that encompasses many emotions, services, and activities. Goodness implies kindness, compassion, service, charity, consoling, understanding, loving, mercy, and truth. Volumes have been written on the subject of goodness, all of which describe high states of self. Compassion, however, must be distinguished from sympathy, which is often mistakenly used interchangeably. Compassion is supportive, uplifting, and positive; it fills the needs of another at the moment. Sympathy, on the other hand, is feeling sorry for ourselves and indulging in our own weaknesses. It drains our energy and emotions and generally comes from the lower self.

Essentially, goodness is the way to give purpose and meaning to life. It is to give service and to contribute to the world for the glorification of our creator. Everyone has a place, a purpose, a role, and a function to fulfill in life. "We must serve in order to receive" is really a natural law, because we cannot consume unless we produce. We were born with natural abilities and talents that were given to us by our maker to serve and complement each other. When all the temperaments blend together in society, each temperament contributes to form a harmonious unity. The weaknesses of one temperament are canceled out by the strengths of another temperament, and so, by working interdependently with each other, humankind is made strong and in balance.

Many people today are insensitive to giving and serving. This is reflected in the marked decline in church attendance and the thousands of local churches that are dying and closing their doors. Someone cleverly stated, "When it comes to serving and giving, many people today will stop at nothing." Many people are more interested in receiving and serving their own self-centered needs. God shaped each of us to serve, give, and share our gifts with others, not for self-centeredness. The world and our ego define greatness in terms of power, material possessions, money, fame, prestige, title, and position. God determines your greatness by how many people you served and not how many people served you. "Who wants to be great must become a servant," states Mark 10:43.

The following famous prayer of St. Francis of Assisi not only reveals goodness, but the healing words are truly a spiritual prescription for seeking balance and harmony in our lives. It is a wonderful prayer for daily meditation.

Lord, make me an instrument of thy peace.
Where there is hatred, let me sow love;
Where there is injury, pardon;
Where there is doubt, faith;
Where there is despair, hope;
Where there is darkness, light;
Where there is sadness, joy;
O Divine Master, grant that I may not so much seek
To be consoled as to console,
To be understood as to understand,
To be loved as to love:
For it is in giving that we receive;
It is in pardoning that we are pardoned;
It is in dying to self that we are born to eternal life.

It is refreshing to know that many individuals and organizations are practicing goodness. The meaning of goodness is the primary function of the international Rotary Club, whose motto is "Service above self." Their four-way test encompasses the essence of goodness and represents the things they think, say, or do:

1. Is it the truth?
2. Is it fair to all concerned?
3. Will it build goodwill and better friendships?
4. Will it be beneficial to all concerned?

The lives of Mahatma Gandhi (1869–1948), Albert Schweitzer (1875–1965), Pope John Paul II (1920–2005), Mother Teresa (1910–1997), and Martin Luther King Jr. (1929–1968) all exemplified pureness of heart and goodness with all its meaning. Each of these people exemplified Christlike features in their lives.

6. Gentleness
A gentle answer turns away wrath but harsh words cause quarrels.
—Proverbs 15:1–2

Gentleness is a high state of mind and is a true virtue in all aspects of life. It should be applied in walking, in talking, in thinking, in action, in writing, in playing, in physical contact, and in all creative works (art, music, performing, etc.). Gentleness implies an easygoing, light-hearted attitude that, in fact, potentiates all spiritual qualities. Our talents and strengths are unique in each individual, and were given to us to share with the world for the glorification of our creator. With gentleness, completion of one's mission and purpose in life will be made natural and easier. A statement of truth once said, "You help yourself by forgetting yourself." To focus exclusively on ourselves produces stress, anxiety, and the fear of failure and rejection. This occurs as a result of a blockage from a free flow of creational spirit.

It is of utmost importance to be gentle with yourself. This is an act of self-forgiveness that eliminates any shame, blame, or guilt. This act allows us to live our lives as we choose, to make our own mistakes, and to learn from these mistakes and life's experiences. In reality, all individuals find it impossible to perfectly maintain a code of conduct consistent with traditional religious beliefs or moral standards established by others. Perceived failures always follow them, producing feelings of guilt, shame, or blame. These feelings, in turn, inhibit one's own awakening, prevent being responsible for one's own mind, and stand in the way of fully accepting yourself. It takes a strong effort to release the control imposed on you by the moral standards and beliefs of others. Once you have released yourself, you are well on your way to mastering the art of self-forgiveness, and you no longer have the need to judge others. Releasing judgment of another's behavior is actually releasing judgment of yourself.

Past events and actions that you may have considered mistakes or failures are only lessons that had to be learned; they give you the opportunity to learn and grow. To label yourself otherwise is judging yourself rather than accepting yourself. Self-acceptance leads to self-love. An abundance of self-love is what you have to give away.

Willingness to be gentle with yourself in all ways, and forgiving yourself, even if you slip, is necessary to be in harmony with all the universal principles. It gives you the right to choose whatever you wish to pursue in life, the right to self-determination, and the right to be treated as the divine being that you are.

7. Humility
True humility and fear of the Lord leads to riches, honor and long life.
—Proverbs 22:4

Humility and meekness are high states of mind. True humility is an attitude of the heart and mind, and consists of knowing one's proper place in life. Self-made men usually find it difficult to accept this attitude. It is never aggressive, boastful, self-aggrandizing, nor controlling. Humility, also called "poor in spirit," is nonjudgmental and low-keyed, and avoids gossip. A humble person never demeans anybody, especially in public. They accept things as they are without demanding, complaining, shaming, or blaming. They are, however, open-minded, teachable, and able to change their minds. Humble people enjoy acceptance and approval from others, but do not seek or have a need of them. Their primary motivation in life is not to impress people with their self-ego, achievements, or false piety, but to serve and surrender to the will of God—in essence, to "let go and let God" guide their path through life. Humility is putting the other person first and having a Christlike attitude, which is his only self-description: "I am gentle and humble at heart" (Matthew 11:29).

Wayne M. Dyer, in his book *Wisdom of the Ages*, writes about some spiritual leaders of the past who typify humility: Alexander Pope (1688–1744), in his poems on solitude, suggested that humility is to live in peace with dignity, unseen and unknown. Lao-Tzu (sixth century BC), who established the basis for the religious practice of Taoism, stated a paradox in the nature of humility, "All streams flow to the ocean because it is lower than they are. Humility gives it its power." Henry David Thoreau (1817–1862), an American writer and nonconformist, related, "Humility like darkness reveals the heavenly lights." Christ proclaimed, "Those who humble themselves will be glorified; those who glorify themselves will be humbled." In the Beatitudes, Christ rewarded humility and meekness: "The poor in spirit shall inherit the kingdom of heaven and the meek shall inherit the earth."

8. Faith
God blesses those who obey him. Happy is the man who puts his trust in the Lord. —Proverbs 16:20

Faith is a high state of believing in the universal world that is governed by God or the almighty universal mind. It is believing in the meaning of Gods' purpose for the existence of the living universe and humanity. It is in believing that we can make contact with this high spiritual mind, that we can make requests, and that we can manifest these requests through this source. In other words, faith is believing in the certainty that what we hope for is waiting for us, even though we cannot see it up ahead.

Faith is impossible to have without a direct experience with God. Relying on the testimony and beliefs of others will never establish true faith and will always leave you with doubt. Faith will come when you ascend to higher energy levels with direct contact with the faster frequencies of spiritual consciousness (spiritual values and the high states of self).

True faith cannot live harmoniously with the lower-frequency states of self, such as hate, chaos, fear, and doubt. These lower vibrational states of self result from a feeling that we are separate from any spiritual energy, when, in reality, that spiritual energy is your true self and a reflection of God. In the higher planes of self we recognize that God is love, and the power of love dominates and directs all living things. This higher state of self will restore you to a place where hate, chaos, fear, and doubt cannot exist and will be dissolved.

No one can oblige you to have faith, nor can anyone force you to love. When you force love, you create resistance or even hate. Trying to force faith leads one most often to doubt and disbelief. Spiritual consciousness is the power that created and supports the universal system. Our own physical body is a part of this system. The universe and our own physical body are creations that are perfectly coordinated in functions and purpose. They are characterized by cooperation, harmony, peace, and flow, which together comprise love, the source of all living things, and are the spirit of God.

Belief in spiritual consciousness is faith whose frequency of energy vibrates so fast that it transcends the capacity to believe only through our five senses. When one accesses the higher states of spiritual consciousness, it should be with privacy and silence. Faith should not be a subject to defend or argue about. That is a waste of time, and can only lead to a low state of ego-bashing, a need to be right, and doubts, which may even produce the inability to access spiritual consciousness. There is truth in an old statement, "Convince a person against his will, and he will be of the same opinion still."

The best method of maintaining contact with your source and high states of self is to meditate daily. Meditation is an excellent practice for reducing stress, relieving fatigue, nourishing the soul, producing a feeling of well-being, and creating a sense of self-control over our lives. This constitutes faith.

9. Self-control, Discipline, and Worthiness
Self-control means controlling the tongue: a quick retort can ruin everything.
—Proverbs 13:3

Self-control is a high state of self that comes from awareness and allows one to essentially avoid confrontations, disagreements, and painful statements, and to accept all temperaments as they are. Anger, hot words, and arguments cause mistakes, and never result in cool judgments. Self-control is using positive statements regarding the undertaking of any activity, and avoiding those who persistently insist on burdening you with their grievances. It leads one to listen more, speak less, think before speaking, and avoid gossip. It teaches one to avoid hyper-needing of anything in life, including love, recognition for achievements, money, or control of others. Your need is always fulfilled by believing in the spiritual world, as noted in the Twenty-third Psalm, "The Lord is my shepherd, I shall not want."

Self-discipline is believing that you can achieve anything that you really desire. This goal can be reached by thinking and imagining that you have already arrived at achieving this goal—being a better golfer or a better musician, losing weight, being free of disease, or any other achievement. It is important to avoid announcing to others negative feelings of fatigue, anxiety, fears, and worries. Stay silent about these feelings rather than having these thoughts radiate a self-fulfilling prophecy. Be a positive-thinking doer rather than a negative-thinking critic, complainer, or explainer.

Self-worthiness is having respect and unconditional love for yourself—as Christ, in his second commandment, said, "Love thy neighbor as thyself." You, therefore, cannot love your neighbor unless you love yourself first. Look upon your body as a gift from your creator given to you as a loan to house your spirit through this life. It is, therefore, a divine gift that you must love, appreciate, and take care of. You are an eternal spirit temporarily harbored in a body, and not a body temporarily harboring a spirit. Eliminate any self-denigrating labels and comments, and let others who do this to you understand privately that you do not care to be identified this way any longer. Finally, choose to change your self-image by viewing your life as an illuminated force of nature that is here for a purpose. It means that you are not going to die until the music in you is played out and you have fulfilled your mission on earth.

Chart 9 describes the spiritual values and high states of self, listing the nine fruit of the spirit listed in Galatians 5:22–23 and the related high states of self. These are essentially the positive thoughts to constantly fill your mind with, to replace the negative low states of self. The memorization and visualization of this chart will be a great tool for meditation and achieving spiritual balance.

Chart 9
Spiritual Values and High States of Self

1. LOVE
The universal synthesizer
Most important and all powerful
Unconditional and all-inclusive
God is love and only responds to love
The two commandments of Christ encompass all aspects of love:
Love your god with all your heart, soul, mind and strength
Love your neighbor as yourself (Matthew 22:35–40)

2. Joy	**3. Peace**	**4. Patience**	**5. Goodness**
Bliss	Calmness	Tolerance	Kindness
Harmony	Relaxation	Acceptance	Compassion
Balance	Silence	Persistence	Service
Enthusiasm	Serenity	Endurance	Charity
Happiness	Meditation	Strong-willed	Consoling
Humor and	Intuitive listening	Long-suffering	Understanding
laughter	Surrendering to	Waiting on God	Mercy
Sharing of	God	Listen more,	Affirmation of
natural gifts	Spiritual	speak less	others
Completion of	insights	Objective	Justice
service	Forgiveness of	observation	Truth and
Fulfillment of	others and self		fairness
purpose			Goodwill and
Joy with family			better friendships
Friends and			Beneficial to
fellowship			others

6. Gentleness

In walk
In talk
In thought
In action
In writing
In playing
In performance
In physical
contact
In completion
of mission
In self-reflection
In self-forgive-
ness (without
shame, blame,
or guilt)

7. Humility

Let go and let
God
Never aggressive
Never self-
aggrandizing
Never arrogant
or boisterous
Never boasting
or bragging
Never blaming,
complaining, or
explaining
Never criticizing
or condemning
Never control-
ling
Never gossiping
Never judgmen-
tal

Always low-
keyed
Always loving
nature
Always avoiding
arguments and
confrontation
Always surren-
der to God
Always grateful
and thankful

8. Faith

Belief in God
Belief in God's
creations
Belief in
purpose
Belief in love
Belief in will
Belief in
guidance
Belief in hope
and abundance

9. Self-control

Awareness
Positive thinking
Listen more,
speak less
Thinking before
speaking
Avoid over-
needing (anyone
or anything)

Self-discipline
Conceive,
believe, and
achieve.

Self-worth
Self-respect
Unconditional
love of self

Low States of Self

The Lord hates the thoughts of the wicked but delights in kind words.
—Proverbs 15:16

Negative emotions and actions are low states of self that are low vibrational energies that emanate from man's ego located in the mind. They are freely chosen by people and are the chief source of most destruction to mankind. Throughout the world, it is known that negative expressions are several times greater in number than positive expressions and high states of mind.

Anger and fear are the root causes of most negative thoughts and actions observed in most people. The choleric- and sanguine-dominant temperaments are more anger-prone, whereas the melancholic- and phlegmatic-dominant temperaments are more fear-prone. Because most people have a more balanced combination of temperaments, a natural predisposition to both anger and fear is exhibited. Chart 10 shows some of the common responses of anger in the four temperaments.

Anger and fear are both destructive and costly to the whole person—body, mind, and spirit. The most destructive forces in humanity involve hate, injury, doubting, despair, suffering, pain, and disease. The prayer of St. Francis of Assisi is truly an effective spiritual prescription to remedy these afflictions.

Dr. LaHaye, in his book *Spirit-Controlled Temperament*, lists sixteen variations for each anger and fear. Many are descriptions that disguise the root cause, which is anger and fear. Chart 11 lists these variations.

Temperaments' Reactions to Anger

Chart 10

I'm right and you're wrong.
Choleric ♠

I'm mad, but let's eat.
Sanguine ♥

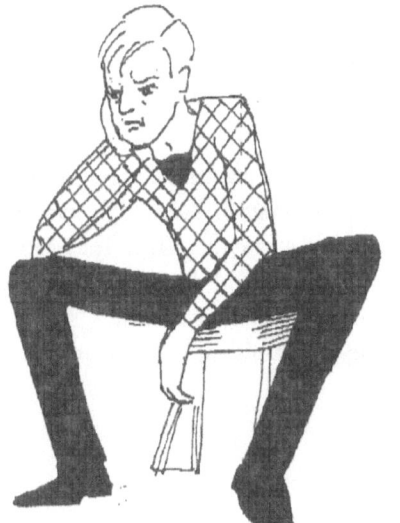

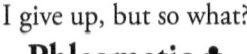

I give up, but so what?
Phlegmatic ♣

Anger and low states of mind—I've got them all. **Melancholic ♦**

Drawings by Virginia Ferrara Twaits

Chart 11
Low States of Self
Variations of Anger and Fear
Freely Chosen from Man's Ego

The following are variations of anger:

Bitterness	Wrath	Criticism
Malice	Hatred	Sarcasm
Clamor	Intolerance	Unforgiveness
Envy	Jealousy	Gossip
Resentment	Attacks	Judgment
	Seditions	Revenge

The following are variations of fear:

Anxiety	Worry	Withdrawal
Doubt	Inferiority	Depression
Timidity	Cowardice	Loneliness
Indecision	Suspicion	Sadness
Superstition	Hesitancy	Haughtiness
Overaggression	Social shyness	Fretting

The spiritual costs of anger and fear prevent us from strengthening our weaknesses by blocking the positive effects of spiritual values and high states of self. Anger and fear keep us from a joyous, happy, and radiant life. They cause one to eventually be thankless, complaining, defeated, and ultimately faithless. "Without faith it is impossible to please God," states Hebrews 11:6.

There are many causes that may lead one to exhibit anger and fear. These include the following:

1. Temperament traits
2. Unfulfilled childhood without love, understanding, acceptance, and discipline
3. Overprotection in childhood, resulting in an inability to cope
4. Anger and disapproval by a dominating parent
5. Traumatic experience in childhood, such as abuse or sexual molestation
6. Negative thinking pattern in family
7. Lack of faith and belief in a superior being

We produce our own fear in today's world of uncertain circumstances. The news media constantly reminds us of possible economic crisis, brutalities, wars, fighting, rioting, violence, abuse, and the threat of nuclear weapons, terrorist attacks, and natural disasters. Fear for ourselves is also prevalent among people—a fear of losing a job or not finding one, and fears of failure, breakdown, and poverty.

The most important and underlying cause of anger and fear is self-centeredness. Fear and anger are born out of selfishness. There is fear of failure or disapproval in your personal involvements, appearance, performance, entertaining others, and so on; these are really expressions of selfishness. The remedy is to think more about others and less about yourself. Biblical revelations are filled with the messages and answers to anger and fear—to trust in the Lord with faith and love. Ninety-five percent of the things we fear and worry about never happen. If they do become a reality, we must do what we can, and God will do what we can't. "God blesses those who obey Him. Happy is the man who puts his trust in the Lord," states Proverbs 16:20.

Changing your attitude by meditating and focusing your mind on the nine fruit of the spirit can turn your thoughts of low states to high states of mind, and "you will receive what you believe"—peace, harmony, health, and happiness.

To live creatively, we must be willing to be a little vulnerable; it is a small risk to be hurt a little. Do not fret, because this will give you a healthy thickness and toughness to your emotional skin—so that you learn to go on living and creating with joy.

PART FIVE

BIRTH OF A NEW ERA

CHAPTER XIII

Holistic and Integrative Medicine

The modern concept of holistic medicine is essentially the study and practice of medicine as it relates to the whole person, which includes the body, mind, and spirit. The resurgence of the Hippocrates theory of the four temperaments was a spark for the birth of holistic and integrative medicine. This was also associated with the reawakening of constitutional medicine, which entails an interest in the association between body build, personality, and predispositions to certain diseases, especially when the person is in an unbalanced state. This led to the development of integrative medicine, which encompasses all of the benefits of the healing arts. These include ancient and modern concepts of healing the whole person—body, mind, and spirit.

During the past century, the practice of clinical medicine and physical diagnosis has been replaced by the advent of modern medicine, which predominantly utilizes the vast new scientific and computerized technologies. This new era of medicine has produced both positive and negative effects. The negative effects have left a void in the spiritual aspects of our society. This has primarily led to health care that has become increasingly impersonal and authoritative in attitude, with rigid administrative controls, and seemingly an orientation toward commercialism. The great values of our highly functional and spiritual people have been subjugated in the name of scientific progress. There is now a quest for the rediscovery, study, and return of ancient traditional practices, values, and wisdom. There is a reawakening of the interest in the values that consider the whole person. People are seeking more knowledge concerning total body care with a more holistic approach, one that encompasses emotional and mental conditions, nutrition, exercise, environmental influences, and belief systems involving the mystical and spiritual forces. They desire health care providers who will listen, console, and encourage their patients to take an active role in the healing process.

The birth of holistic and integrative medicine is a relatively new aspect of health care and patient management that meets these desires. Besides psychotherapy and counseling, it utilizes the benefits of many alternative methods of therapy, including massage, physical and spa therapy, hypnosis, yoga, imaging, music, art, aromatherapy, and meditation. Increasing numbers of health care providers are now incorporating many of these alternative therapies into their practices. A growing number of hospitals in the United States are offering alternative and complementary care alongside conventional treatment. There is a greater degree of acceptance and approval by conventional medicine as more favorable outcomes of holistic medicine are reported in the scientific literature. More scientific literature is revealing that in many cases a more conservative holistic approach to patient care works as well as conventional approaches, with a tremendous added safety factor. Dr. Dean Ornish, MD, in his book on heart research, showed that coronary artery disease can be successfully treated in many cases using a holistic approach with a nutritional low-fat diet, exercise, yoga, and group support. Andrew Weil, MD, is a leading advocate of alternative medicine, and is director of the well-known program in integrative medicine at the University of Arizona. He was one of the first to change medical education to include information on alternative therapies, mind-body interactions, healing, and other subjects not currently emphasized in the training of physicians. He is the author of nine books on these subjects, which include *Spontaneous Healing,* one of his several international bestsellers.

There are many recent positive trends that support holistic medicine in the medical arena. Medical schools are inviting holistic physicians to lecture or to develop programs in the schools to complement the more conventional curriculum. The National Institutes of Health has developed an office to support and research holistic and alternative medicine practices. With the current trends in medical education, the changing needs and expectations of a more informed public, and the increasing scientific validation of holistic approaches, the coming of age of holistic and integrative medicine is assured. The new frontier of health care and human awareness has arrived.

There are basic differences in the philosophies of conventional and holistic medicine. Conventional medicine is more focused on diagnosis and treatment of specific diseases using scientifically proven techniques and modalities. This focus mainly involves interest in drugs, surgery, and radiation, as well as various uses of light, lasers, and chemotherapy. Little consideration is given to the healthy whole person and the prevention of disease. Holistic medicine is more focused on prevention of disease and maintenance of health by encouraging a balance of the body systems—mind, body, and spirit. Holistic medical practitioners see all of these factors as interrelated, producing a state of wholeness called holism. Their premise is that an imbalance or disharmony in any of these areas stresses the body to ultimately produce sickness or illness. Alternative medicine uses a wide range of therapies to boost the body's own defenses to restore balance. It also believes that natural healing entails a positive attitude, and that a negative attitude creates stresses that have a debilitating effect on the vascular, endocrine, and immune systems. The medical community has acknowledged that a positive attitude and belief system can play a vital role in overcoming disease and maintaining good health. There is a consensus that alternative medicine is rapidly becoming popular worldwide, and that the health insurance industry is beginning to consider covering alternative treatments. There is still considerable resistance for both alternative and conventional medicine to integrate in both thought and treatment. Some states have passed laws that protect holistic providers from potential harassment by opposing conventional practitioners. Ultimately, the integration will be needed in order to give patients the best of all fields of study.

CHAPTER XIV

The Integration of Alternative Therapies

There is growing acceptance of alternative healing methods of treatment being integrated into the practice of conventional medicine, referred to as holistic, complementary, or integrative medicine. Many of the modalities considered in alternative medicine have long been recognized as natural and desirable features of human nature. I have grouped them as minor or other modalities of alternative therapies, and include such examples as hypnotherapy, music and sound, art and color, humor, and pets. These subjects, however, are now being studied scientifically, and have proven to be effective in the healing practices.

Conventional medicine has viewed many of these practices with skepticism, but in the past few decades, these modalities classified as alternative medicine are increasingly being integrated into conventional medicine. A major group of alternative therapies are now seriously being considered and incorporated into the new field of holistic and integrative medicine. Some are presently being investigated and funded for research by the National Institutes of Health. The major and most popular subjects of alternative medicine are discussed in the following section.

Popular Modalities of Alternative Therapies

1. Acupuncture

This modality has recently become a popular alternative therapy. It is an ancient Chinese method that claims to restore health, balance, and vitality. This is proclaimed to be achieved by directing the flow of energy through the body's meridians. This method uses the insertion of very fine needles at different points along the meridians of the body to restore health and balance. Acupuncture has been shown to stimulate the immune system, the circulation and blood pressure, and the heart rate and rhythm. It also stimulates gastric secretions, and the production of blood cells and a variety of bodily hormones. Acupuncture has been claimed to effectively block chronic pain in conditions such as arthritis, bursitis, headache, athletic injuries, and post-traumatic and post-surgical pain. It has also been found to be effective in a wide variety of mind-body disorders. Acupuncture is believed to work through its influence on the electromagnetic field and by altering the chemical neurotransmitters in the body. The acupuncturist may also advise the adjunctive use of other healing techniques, such as diet, exercise, meditation, and a change in one's belief system. Peace, harmony, and balance produce a free flow of energy that leads to physical, emotional, and spiritual well-being.

2. Aromatherapy

Aromatherapy means treatment using scents. It is a holistic treatment of caring for the body by using scents from botanical oils, such as rose, lemon, lavender, and peppermint. These essential oils are exposed to the body by massage or inhalation, and may be diffused to scent an entire room. The many essential oils are known to have distinctive therapeutic, psychological, and physiological properties, and invigorate the entire body. Aromatherapy is one of the fastest-growing fields in alternative medicine, and is widely used in hospitals and treatment centers. For maximum benefit, the essential oils must be extracted from their natural sources, because synthetically made oils do not work.

Aromatherapy is slowly getting into the mainstream for its beneficial effects. It is being incorporated in places such as new buildings, offices, and banks.

3. Biofeedback

Biofeedback is based on the premise that we have an innate ability and potential to influence the autonomic nervous system function through the exertion of our will and mind. This has been demonstrated in some people who can produce a profound temperature difference in their hands or feet, or who can block the pain of colitis or neuritis, by controlling the heart rate and blood pressure, preventing them from increasing under stress.

Biofeedback received much skepticism in the past, but is now recognized to be effective in certain individuals who suffer from migraine headaches, asthma, and other disorders.

4. Chelation

Chelation has been used widely for the treatment of arteriosclerosis and other chronic degenerative diseases involving the circulatory system. It has been claimed to relieve arteriosclerosis with associated pain in the lower extremities and angina pain. The active principle is abbreviated EDTA (ethylene-diamine-tetra-acetic acid), which is a synthetic amino acid. When EDTA is used systemically, it is thought to remove certain metallic catalysts from the body; this is called chelation. This purportedly has an antioxidant effect that initiates healing by reversing the damage in the body. It was initially used in the 1940s for heavy metal poisoning, hypercalcemia, and digitalis toxicity, and later became popular for the treatment of arteriosclerosis.

5. Guided Imagery and Visualization

Imagination and visualization are potent healers long overlooked by Western medicine. Imagery can relieve pain, speed healing, and aid in the recovery from a vast number of ailments including depression, impotence, allergies, and asthma. The power of the mind to influence the body is remarkable. Imagery is the language that the mind uses to communicate with the body. It is extremely useful in mind-body healing. It is beneficial when imaging is positive, but can be harmful to the body when it is negative. For example, worry exists only in the imagination, and can have a negative effect on the body's physiology, producing a variety of ailments, such as acne, headaches, and infections. Your thoughts have a direct influence on the way you feel and behave. If you learn to direct and control your own images, you directly help your body, and they become a powerful tool to combat stress, tension, and anxiety. Imaging for a few minutes two or three times a day is highly recommended. For this purpose, imaging does not limit itself to visualization, but can include sounds, tastes, smells, or combinations of these. Imaging has been used since ancient civilization. It is applied in all events of life, such as sports and leadership, and to affirm oneself in all activities and challenges. It can help by creating a comfort zone, so that when the actual situation occurs, you can meet it without fear. Virtually everyone can successfully use imagery. It is a practice of the high states of self, especially patience, persistence, and self-control.

6. Herbal Medicine

Herbs have been used since ancient times to heal the body, clear the mind, clear the colon, and soothe the soul. St. Luke, one of the authors of the New Testament, was a physician and a noted herbalist who believed there was an effective herb for every bodily ailment or disease. Such herbs are administered by ingestion or topically in ointments, plasters, or solutions.

It is estimated that 80 percent of the world's population has used herbal medicine for some aspect of primary health care. Herbal medicine is a major component of traditional medicine and a primary source for synthesizing the active ingredients of modern drugs. It is the common element in ayurveda, homeopathy, naturopathy, and American Indian medicine. Western herbalism is today primarily a system of folk medicine. Examples of popular herbs used today include St. John's wart, ginseng, and ginkgo biloba.

7. Homeopathy

Homeopathy is already incorporated to a large extent in modern medicine. The principle is that those substances that are poisonous to the body in large doses can be very beneficial in small doses. Homeopathy treats the body as a whole and helps it to heal itself. The object is prevention by strengthening the body's defenses. Homeopathy essentially means treating like with like. Vaccination therapy is a good example of homeopathy.

8. Chiropractic

The chiropractic approach deals with treating the musculoskeletal system to bring balance to the body's structure and nervous system. Chiropractors contend that manual adjustments of bones, joints, and especially the spine will bring the body back into alignment, which supports mental, emotional, and spiritual health. They view their hands as actual healing instruments that contact energy and reflex centers that support and help integrate the systems of the body, so that it can heal itself.

Chiropractic is receiving wider acceptance for the treatment of low back pain and headache. It is rapidly growing in popularity, and chiropractors are now the third-largest group of healing providers in the United States, after medical doctors and dentists. Most insurance now pays part of the cost of chiropractic, and there is increasing collaboration with medical doctors.

9. Hydrotherapy

Hydrotherapy is the use of water in the treatment of disease. Hydrothermal therapy uses the effects of temperature in hot baths, saunas, and wraps.

Hydrotherapy has been used for centuries in ancient Rome, China, and Japan. Its effects are both mechanical and thermal. There are many methods of applying hydrotherapy, which include baths, saunas, douches, wraps, and packs. The effects are hot and cold stimuli, protracted heat effects, and mechanical pressure effects of water and the sensation it gives. The effects of water can stimulate the immune system, stimulate the production of stress hormone, invigorate circulation and digestion, and lessen pain sensitivity.

In general, heat calms and soothes the body while slowing down activity of the internal organs. Cold stimulates and invigorates the body and increases activity of the internal organs. People with stress are benefited by hot showers or baths. People with fatigue, depression, and stress are benefited by a warm shower or bath followed by a cold shower to invigorate and stimulate the body and mind.

Suspension in water produces weightlessness and a relief from gravity. The massagelike feeling of running water stimulates touch receptors of the skin, stimulates circulation, and relaxes tight muscles of the body. For these reasons, most people prefer the massaging effect and the reduction of stress experienced with whirlpools over still baths.

10. Massage Therapy

Massage therapy is the systematized manipulation of soft tissues for the purpose of normalizing them. It is primarily done by the use of hands, but may also use forearms, elbows, and feet. The benefits include increased ability of the body to heal itself, an increase in health and well-being, conveyance of a sense of caring, and relief of muscle soreness. In addition to decreasing anxiety and respiratory rate, it stimulates the immune system, as evidenced by an increase in white cell and T-cell activity, diminishing pain (as in cancer patients), and alleviating depression. It has been shown to hasten recovery after abdominal surgery, to lower blood pressure in hypertension, to reduce heart rate, and, in general, to improve patients both mentally and physically. There are several types of massage therapy, including reflexology, which is the use of thumb and finger pressure on reflex points of the feet. All the various types of massage assist in achieving balance within the body.

11. Meditation

Meditation is an activity that pleasantly anchors the mind to the present moment to produce calm and peace. The benefits to the body, mind, and spirit have been discussed in the section on mind reorientation. There are two basic approaches to meditation:

- Concentration meditation focuses on breathing, visualization, or a sound (mantra) in order to still the mind and make contact with the higher self.
- Mindfulness meditation opens the attention and awareness of the continuously passing parade of sensations, feelings, images, thoughts, sounds, and smells, while maintaining a calm, clear, nonreactive state of mind.

Meditation is a proven alternative therapy that doctors are prescribing to lower blood pressure and to relieve angina pain, asthmatic attacks, insomnia, and stress. It is a safe and simple method to balance the physical, emotional, and mental states. It is rooted in all religions known for thousands of years, and is accepted to alleviate suffering and promote healing.

12. Nutrition and Vitamin and Mineral Therapy

This subject is huge in accumulated knowledge, research, and scientific discoveries over the past century that is beyond the scope of this book. Suffice it to say that the knowledge and application of proper nutrition, including all the essential vitamins and minerals, are extremely important in the prevention and healing of disease for health, happiness, and longevity. The nutrients of the body are water, carbohydrates, protein, fat, and the micronutrients that represent the essential vitamins and minerals. The Federal Drug Administration (FDA) has arbitrarily established the recommended daily allowances (RDAs) of the micronutrients to prevent diseases. However, an increased daily amount may be necessary to maintain health and can be obtained from sufficient ingestion of the proper nutritious foods and by taking supplements.

13. Yoga

Yoga is a method of self-improvement that is one of the best means to attain one's full potential, eventually producing bliss, peace, and increased psychic powers. It was developed in India several thousand years ago. Meditation with yoga is the most popular alternative treatment among doctors, other professionals, and laypeople. Yoga works on the mind and body at the same time. It is interdependent, and no other system of therapy does this. Yoga postures and breathing exercises deal with the body, but also affect the brain and mind at the same time. Modern science provides wonders in the external environment. Yoga provides vitality, rejuvenation, and peace of mind in the internal environment. Yoga is the applied science of mind and body, which brings balance for health. It is a philosophy of body, mind, and spirit.

In India, yoga includes a set of ethical imperatives and moral aspects that include diet, exercise, and meditation. It enhances health, treats chronic diseases, and reduces stress. Yoga consists of a three-pronged attack: (1) yoga postures, which strengthen the body; (2) breathing controls, which create chemical and emotional controls; and (3) mind affirmation—the power of prayer and meditation. All three of these features combined produce powerful healing effects and the basic harmony of life. There are several types of yoga with different focuses. The basic concept in yoga is that most diseases are caused by reduced immunity due to insufficient life forces, which are corrected by yoga.

Other Modalities of Alternative Therapies

The following subjects of alternative therapy have been selected for mention here although they are not the most common alternative therapies at this time. Some have been utilized and commonly recognized as natural features and desires of human nature. As yet, they have not received special research or scientific investigation. They, nevertheless, are considered as important as adjunctive therapy in the healing process and in spiritual values for achieving health and high states of self. These modalities of healing include hypnotherapy, music and sound therapy, art and color therapy, neurolinguistic programming (NLP), pet therapy, light therapy, spiritual healing, ayurveda, and reiki.

CHAPTER XV

Holism and Hope for a Better World

It is becoming more evident that modern medicine, while increasing the lifespan of people, has not provided the basic human needs or significantly curtailed human suffering and problems of the world. Science, though it classifies and explains mechanisms and how things work, does not explain why, nor clarify meanings and purpose in life.

During the past century, science and technology have rapidly advanced and made great discoveries that have benefited humanity and provided people with miraculous diagnostic and therapeutic modalities in the medical arena. These developments have saved lives and increased longevity. All fields of medicine and surgery have experienced the benefits of these dramatic changes. This is especially true in fields that deal with the aging process, extension of life, and in the cardiovascular, musculoskeletal, neurological, urological, ocular, and auditory systems. Despite the huge scientific advances, civilizations have experienced more miseries, fears, and conflicts, along with the quest for more worldly goods than in any other period of history. People sense a spiritual void and are searching for meaning, truths, values, and purpose in life. This need for understanding and fulfillment of mind and spirit is evident in the new era, and in the birth of holistic and integrative medicine. This concept encompasses the total evaluation, diagnosis, and treatment of the whole person—body, mind, and spirit.

The Hippocratic temperament theory has reawakened an interest in the associations of temperament, physical characteristics, and a predisposition to certain diseases. Awareness that disease and suffering occurs primarily in the unbalanced temperament has led to a search for ways to promote our strengths and to strengthen our weaknesses.

Dr. Bruce Lipton, in his book *The Biology of Belief*, demonstrates scientifically that positive emotions and beliefs correct negative and harmful influences on all aspects of life. He affirms that removing negative, outmoded, and detrimental beliefs from the subconscious mind, and replacing them with a positive belief system, is essential to obtain and maintain a healthy balance in life.

Meditation, with thoughts of spiritual values of high states, will accomplish this goal over time. We have learned that we are not bound by inherent and environmental factors that determine our fate in life without any self-responsibility. Recent research has confirmed that by choice we can balance our lives, prevent disease and suffering, and enjoy a life of health, happiness, and longevity.

In summary, life can be equated in a simplistic manner to a deck of cards. We are dealt a specific hand without our choice, usually consisting of a mixture of strong and weak cards (such as temperaments). We must accept the hand we are dealt and the responsibility to manage it successfully. With this knowledge, our experiences, and a belief system, we can manage our hand to achieve our desired goals in life with balance and the maximum potential for health, happiness, and longevity.

This book covers a broad spectrum of natural information that is not easily digested in one reading. However, I believe it will be helpful as a reference and review of the basic truths of our existence in life. It represents many personal experiences and meanings, which certainly must be reflected in most people. The proper management of the cards dealt to us (temperament blends) involves an integral understanding of body, mind, and spirit. The quest for an in-depth knowledge of this trilogy has given rise to a new concept of medical practice—referred to as integrative and holistic medicine.

The considerations and needs of the whole person should enhance international fellowship and promote a better understanding of humanity and world cultures. This can lead to a universal unity with spiritual values of high states to produce a balance in humanity with resultant health, harmony, purpose, and peace throughout the world.

Hopefully the transition taking place today from conventional medicine to holistic medicine will be facilitated by the inspired information presented in this book.

BIBLIOGRAPHY

INTRODUCTION

Behe, M. J. *Darwin's Black Box*. New York: Simon & Schuster, 1996.

Childs, G. *Understanding Your Temperament*. London: Sophia Books, 1995.

Freud, S. *Introductory Lectures to Psychoanalysis*. New York: Boni & Liveright, 1920.

Kretschmer, E. *Physique and Character*. New York: Copper Square, 1936.

LaHaye, T. *Spirit-Controlled Temperament*. Wheaton, IL: Tyndale House, 1992.

————. *Transformed Temperaments*. Wheaton, IL: Tyndale House, 1971.

————. *Why You Act the Way You Do*. Wheaton, IL: Tyndale House, 1984.

Leman, K. *The Real You*. Grand Rapids, MI: Fleming Revell, 2002.

Lipton, B. *The Biology of Belief*. Santa Rosa, CA: Mountain of Love/Elite Books, 2005.

Littauer, F. *Personality Plus*. Grand Rapids, MI: Fleming Revell, 1983.

————. *Your Personality Tree*. Dallas, TX: Word Publishing, 1986.

Minirth, F., MD, and P. Meier, MD. *Happiness Is a Choice*. Grand Rapids, MI: Fleming Revell, 1994.

Montgomery, S. *People Patterns: A Modern Guide to the Four Temperaments*. Del Mar, CA; Archer Publications, 2002.

Rolfe, R. *The Four Temperaments*. New York: Marlowe and Company, 2002.

Sheldon, W. H. *The Varieties of Human Physique*. New York: Harper & Row, 1940.

————. *The Varieties of Temperament*. New York: Harper & Row, 1942.

Tournier, Paul. *The Whole Person in a Broken World*. New York: Harper & Row, 1947.

Watson, L. *Supernature: A Natural History of the Supernatural*. London: Hodder and Stoughton, 1973.

Wrzaszczak, C. *Know Your Temperament*. St. Louis: The Queen's Work, 1960.

CHAPTER I

Berens, L. V. *Understanding Yourself and Others, An Introduction to Temperament*. Huntington Beach, CA: Telos Publications, 2000.

Childs, G. *Understanding Your Temperament*. London: Sophia Books, 1995.

Hock, C., Rev. *The Four Temperaments*. [Pamphlet.] Milwaukee: Bruce Publications, 1954.

Keirsey, D., and M. Bates. *Please Understand Me.* Del Mar, CA: Prometheus Nemesis Publishing, 1984.

LaHaye, T. *Spirit-Controlled Temperament.* Wheaton, IL: Tyndale House, 1992.

———. *Transformed Temperament.* Wheaton, IL: Tyndale House, 1971.

———. *Why You Act the Way You Do.* Wheaton, IL: Tyndale House, 2002.

Leman, K. *The Real You.* Grand Rapids, MI: Fleming Revell, 2002.

Littauer, F. *Personality Plus.* Grand Rapids, MI: Fleming Revell, 1983.

———. *Your Personality Tree.* Dallas, TX: Word Publishing, 1986.

Meyers, L. *The Myers-Briggs Type Indicator.* Palo Alto, CA: Consulting Psychologists Press, 1985.

Montgomery, S. *People Patterns: A Modern Guide to the Four Temperaments.* Del Mar, CA: Archer Publications, 2002.

Rolfe, R. *The Four Temperaments.* New York: Marlowe & Company, 2002.

CHAPTER II

Berens, L. V. *Understanding Yourself and Others, An Introduction to Temperament.* Huntington Beach, CA: Telos Publications, 2000.

Childs, G. *Understanding Your Temperament.* London: Sophia Books, 1995.

Hock, C., Rev. *The Four Temperaments.* [Pamphlet.] Milwaukee: Bruce Publications, 1954.

Keirsey, D., and M. Bates. *Please Understand Me.* Del Mar, CA: Prometheus Nemesis Publishing, 1984.

LaHaye, T. *Spirit-Controlled Temperament.* Wheaton, IL: Tyndale House, 1992.

———. *Transformed Temperament.* Wheaton, IL: Tyndale House, 1971.

———. *Why You Act the Way You Do.* Wheaton, IL: Tyndale House, 2002.

Leman, K. *The Real You.* Grand Rapids, MI: Fleming Revell, 2002.

Littauer, F. *Personality Plus.* Grand Rapids, MI: Fleming Revell, 1983.

———. *Your Personality Tree.* Dallas, TX: Word Publishing, 1986.

Meyers, L. *The Myers-Briggs Type Indicator.* Palo Alto, CA: Consulting Psychologists Press, 1985.

Montgomery, S. *People Patterns: A Modern Guide to the Four Temperaments.* Del Mar, CA: Archer Publications, 2002.

Rolfe, R. *The Four Temperaments.* New York: Marlowe & Company, 2002.

CHAPTER III

Littauer, F. *Personality Plus.* Grand Rapids, MI: Fleming Revell, 1983.

———. *After the Wedding Comes a Marriage.* Grand Rapids, MI: Fleming Revell, 1981.

CHAPTER IV

Davenport, C. B. *Body Build, Its Development and Inheritance.* Washington, DC: Carnegie Institute of Washington Publications, 1930.

Kretschmer, E. *Physique and Character.* New York: Cooper Square, 1970.

Sheldon, W. H. *The Varieties of Human Physique.* New York: Harper & Row, 1946.

Spranger, E. *Types of Men.* [Trans. P. J. W. Pigors.] New York: G. E. Stechert Company, 1928.

Paterson, D. G., J. A. Harris, C. M. Jackson, P. G. Paterson, and R. E. Scammon. *The Measurement of Man.* Minneapolis: University of Minnesota Press, 1930.

CHAPTER V

Cabot, P. S. The Relationship between Characteristics of Personality and Physique in Adolescents. *Genetic Psychological Monogram,* Vol. 20, No.1, 1938.

Farr, C. B. Bodily Structure, Personality and Reaction Types. *American Journal of Psychiatry* 84:231–244, 1927.

Paterson, D. G., J. A. Harris, C. M. Jackson, P. G. Paterson, and R. E. Scammon. *The Measurement of Man.* Minneapolis: University of Minnesota Press, 1930.

Sheldon, W. H. *The Varieties of Human Physique—An Introduction to Constitutional Psychology.* New York: Harper Brothers Publishing, 1940.

CHAPTER VI

Abravanel, E., MD, and E. King. *Dr. Abravanel's Body Type Diet and Lifetime Nutrition Plan.* New York: Bantam Books, 1984.

Bieler, H. G., MD. *Food Is Your Best Medicine.* New York: Vintage Books, 1965.

Carrel, A. *Man, the Unknown.* New York: Harper & Row, 1933.

Cheraskin, E., MD, W. Ringsdorf Jr., MD, MS. *Psychodietetics. Food as the Key to Emotional Health.* New York: Bantam Books, 1978.

Cleave, T. L., M.R.C.P. *The Saccharine Disease: Conditions Caused by the Taking of Refined Carbohydrates, Such as Sugar and White Flour.* New Canaan, CT: Kean Publishing, 1974.

Clymer, R., and MD Swinburne. *Diet: A Key to Health.* Philadelphia: Franklin Publishing, 1966.

D'Adamo, P. J., MD, and C. Whitney. *Eat Right for Your Type.* New York: Putnam & Sons, 1996.

Eaton, S., MD Boyd, and M. Shustak. *The Paleolithic Prescription: A Program of Diet and Exercise and Design for Living.* New York: Harper & Row, 1974.

Hall, R. H., PhD. *Food for Naught: The Decline in Nutrition.* New York: Vintage Books, 1974.

Howell, E., MD, *Enzyme Nutrition: The Food Enzyme Concept.* Wayne, NJ: Avery Publishing Group, 1985.

Jarvis, D. C., MD. Folk Medicine, and G. E. R. Lloyd, Eds. *Hippocratic Writings.* New York: Penguin Books, 1978.

Rolfe, R. *The Four Temperaments.* New York: Marlowe & Company, 2002.

Watson, G., MD. *Nutrition and Your Mind: The Psychochemical Response.* New York: Bantam Books, 1974.

Winkless, N., and I. Browning. *Climate and the Affairs of Man.* Burlington, VT: Fraser Publishing, 1975.

CHAPTER VII

Darwin, F., Ed. *Charles Darwin, Life and Letters.* London: Charles Murray, 1888. Reprinted by Penguin Books, London, 1965.

Hippocrates. *On Ancient Medium, The Genius Works of Hippocrates.* [Trans. F. Adams.] New York: Wm. Wood Publishing, 1985.

Jung, C. *Psychological Types.* New York: Warner Books, 1989.

Keirsey, D., and M. Bates. *Please Understand Me.* Del Mar, CA: Prometheus Nemesis Publishing, 1984.

Kretschmer, E. *Physique and Character.* New York: Copper Square, 1936.

LaHaye, T. *Transformed Temperaments.* Wheaton, IL: Tyndale House, 1971.

Meyers, I. B. *Introduction to Types,* 5th ed. Palo Alto, CA: Consulting Psychologists Press, 1993.

Rolfe, R. *The Four Temperaments.* New York: Harper & Row, 2002.

Sheldon, W. H. *The Varieties of Temperament.* New York: Harper & Row, 1942.

CHAPTER VIII

Andreole, T. E. *Cecil Essentials of Medicine,* 6th ed. Philadelphia: M. B. Saunders, 2004.

Bolognia, J. L. *Dermatology.* [Two volumes.] Mosley Publishing, 2003.

Bryant, J. *The Carnivorous and Herbivorous Types of Man.* Boston: Boston Medical & Surgical Journal, 1914–1915.

DiGiovanni, A. *Clinical Commentaries Deduced from the Morphology of the Human Body*. New York: J. J. Eyre, 1919.

Draper, G. *Human Constitution: A Consideration of Its Relationship to Disease*. New York: Saunders Co., 1914.

———. *Man as a Complete Organism*. New York: New York State Journal of Medicine, 1934.

Edlund, M. *The Body Clock Advantage*. Avon, MS: Adams Media Corporation, 2003.

Feigenbaum, H., and D. Howat. The Relation between Physical Constitution and the Incidence of Disease. *Journal of Clinical Investigation*, 13(1):121–138, 1934.

Hay, L. L. *You Can Heal Your Life*. Carlsbad, CA: Hay House, 1984.

Kretschmer, E. *Physique and Character*. New York: Copper Square, 1956.

Limmer, E. *The Body Language of Illness*. Liberty Lake, WA: Freedom Press, 1995.

Merck Manual of Medical Information. Whithouse Station, NJ: Merck Research Laboratories, 2003.

Pearl, R. *Constitution and Health*. London: Kegan, Trench, and Trubner, 1933.

Rippy, E. L. *Physical Types and Their Relation to Disease*. Dallas, TX: Dallas Medical Journal, 1936.

Sarno, J. E., MD. *Mind, Body Prescriptions*. New York: Warner Books, 1998.

Tournier, Paul. *The Healing of Persons: Temperaments*. New York: Harper & Row, 1965.

CHAPTER IX

Browsword, A. *It Takes All Types*. Herndon, VA: Baytree Publication Company, 1987.

Canfield, S., and M. V. Hansen. *A Second Helping of Chicken Soup for the Soul*. Deerfield, CA: Health Communications, Inc., 1999.

Covey, S. R. *The Seven Habits of Highly Effective People*. New York: Simon & Schuster, 1989.

Fontana, D. *Know Who You Are, Be What You Want*. New York: HarperCollins, 1997.

Glen, C. W. *Using Type to Enhance Mutual Understanding*. Gainesville, FL: Center for Applications of Psychological Type, 1995.

Hartzler, Margaret. *Using Type in Career Counseling*. Gaithersburg, VA: MD Type Researchers, Inc., 1985.

Hay, L. L. *Letters to Louise*. Carlsbad, CA: Hay House, 1999.

Hirsh, S. K., and J. M. Kummerow. *Introduction to Type in Organizations.* Palo Alto, CA: Consulting Psychologists Press, 1990.

Pearman, R. R. *Hardwired Leadership. Unleashing the Power of Personality to Become a New Millennium Leader.* Palo Alto, CA: Davies-Black, 1998.

Peck, M. S., MD. *A World Waiting to Be Born.* New York: Bantam Books, 1993.

Rolfe, R. *The Four Temperaments.* New York: Marlowe & Company, 2002.

———. *The Seven Secrets of Successful Parents.* Chicago: Contemporary Books, 1997.

Tieger, P. D. *Do What You Are.* New York: Little, Brown, 1992.

CHAPTER X

Carrel, A. *Man, the Unknown.* New York: Penguin Books, 1933.

Childre, D., and H. Martin, with D. Beech. *The Heart Math Solution.* San Francisco: Harper Publishing, 1999.

Chopra, D., MD. *Ageless Body, Timeless Mind.* New York: Harmony Books, 1993.

Freud, S. *The Standard Edition of the Complete Psychological Works of Sigmund Freud.* London: Hogarth Press, 1957.

King James Quick Reference Bible. Nashville, TN: Thomas Nelson, 2000.

Lipton, B. *The Biology of Belief.* Santa Rosa, CA: Mountain of Love/Elite Books, 2005.

Tournier, Paul. *The Healing of Persons.* New York: Harper & Row, 1965.

———. *The Meaning of Persons.* New York: Harper & Row, 1957.

CHAPTER XI

Borysenko, J., PhD. *The Power of the Mind to Heal.* Carlsbad, CA: Hay House, 1994.

Davies, P. *The Mind of God.* New York: Simon & Schuster, 1992.

Dines, J. *Secrets of High States.* Belvedere, CA: James Dines & Company, 2005.

Dossey, L., MD. *Healing Words: The Power of Prayer and the Practice of Medicine.* San Francisco: Harper & Co., 1993.

Dyer, W. W. *Manifest Your Destiny.* New York: HarperCollins, 1997.

———. *Real Magic.* New York: HarperCollins, 1992.

———. *There Is a Spiritual Solution to Every Problem.* New York: HarperCollins, 2001.

———. *Wisdom of the Ages.* New York: HarperCollins, 1998.

———. *You'll See It When You Believe It.* New York: HarperCollins, 1989.

———. *Your Shared Self.* New York: HarperCollins, 1995.

Hill, N. *Grow Rich!—With Peace of Mind.* New York: FawcettCrest, 1967.

Levin, M. *Meditation.* New York: DK Publishing, 2002.

McTaggart, L. *The Field.* New York: HarperCollins, 2001.

Moore, T. *Education of the Heart.* New York: HarperCollins, 1996.

Pagels, H. R. *The Cosmic Code: Quantum Physics as the Language of Nature.* New York: Simon & Schuster, 1982.

Rolfe, R., S. D., M.A. *The Four Temperaments.* New York: Marlowe & Company, 2002.

Swindall, C. *Wisdom for the Way: Wise Words for Busy People.* Nashville, TN: Thomas Nelson Publishing, 2001.

Taylor, S. *Quantum Success.* Carlsbad, CA: Hay House, 2006.

Tournier, P. *A Doctor's Casebook in the Light of the Bible.* New York: Harper & Row, 1959.

———. *Reflections.* New York: Harper & Row, 1976.

Urban, H. *Life's Greatest Lessons.* New York: Simon & Schuster, 1992.

Warren, R. *The Purpose-Driven Life.* Grand Rapids, MI: Zondervan, 2002.

Wilson, E. O. *On Human Nature.* Cambridge, MA: Harvard University Press, 1978.

Chapter XII

Graham, B. *Peace with God, The Secret of Happiness.* Nashville, TN: Thomas Nelson Publishing, 1953.

Krupf, R. N. *Evil and Evolution, A Theory.* Eugene, OR: Wipf and Stock, 2000.

Lewis, C. S. *Mere Christianity.* New York: HarperCollins, 1953.

———. *Readings for Meditation and Reflection.* San Francisco: HarperCollins, 1992.

Lund, M. *Healing the Whole Person, the Whole Planet.* Hillsboro, CA: Beyond Publishing/Spirit Speaks Publishing, 1988.

McMillen, S. I., MD. *None of These Diseases.* Westwood, NJ: Fleming Revell, 1943.

Ornish, D., MD. *Reversing Heart Disease.* New York: Ballantine Books, 1990.

Oschman, J. L. *Vibrational Medicine, Energy Medicine: The Scientific Basis.* Edinburgh: Harcourt, 2000.

Prince, D. *God's Remedy for Rejection.* New Kensington, PA: Whitaker House, 1993.

Schucman, H., and W. Thetford. *A Course in Miracles*, 2nd ed. Mill Valley, CA: Public Foundation for Inner Peace, 1992.

CHAPTER XIII

Chopra, D., MD. *The Book of Secrets: Unlocking the Hidden Dimensions of Your Life*. New York: Harmony Books, 2004.

Hay, L. L. *Colors and Numbers*. Carlsbad, CA: Hay House, 1999.

Horrigan, B. J. *Voices of Integrative Medicine: Conversations and Encounters*. St. Louis, MO: Churchill Livingston, 2003.

Tournier, P. *Guilt and Grace*. New York: Harper & Row, 1962.

Weil, A., MD. *Spontaneous Healing*. New York: Random House, 2000.

Chapter XIV

Church, D., ed. *Healing the Heart of the World*. Santa Rosa, CA: Elite Books, 2005.

Dossey, L., MD. *Meaning and Medicine*. New York: Bantam Books, 1991.

Horrigan, B. *Voices of Integrative Medicine*. St. Louis: Churchill Livingston Publishers, 2003.

Lipton, B. *The Biology of Belief*. Santa Rosa, CA: Mountain of Love/Elite Books, 2005.

Prophet, E. C., and P. Spadaro. *Your Seven Energy Centers. A Holistic Approach to Physical, Emotional and Spiritual Vitality*. Corwin Springs, MT: Summit University Press, 2000.

Tournier, P. *The Whole Person in a Broken World*. New York: Harper & Row, 1947.